Bruce Mclean

Five Decades of Sculpture

With an essay by Mel Gooding and commentary by Bruce McLean

Statements on Sculpture (= a sculpture)

'Let us forget things and consider only the relationships between them.'

Georges Braque

What is sculpture? To place some thing some where.

Not the thing itself (alone) but the where it is placed (together in space and time)

When it is placed time is present at all times.

The thing and its presence where it is placed are inscribed in time
(where and when else could it be?)

No thing is timeless.

The presence of the thing where it is placed signifies time (among other things
sculptural: sculptural time is multiple and multivalent.)

Time is the ultimate sculpture.

***

To photograph some thing some where may be a sculptural act: the thing
photographed may be the sculpture, the photograph the trace or record
(partial, necessarily) of the sculpture. The photograph may be a sculpture.

***

Not every thing is sculpture: determination and intent are components of sculpture.

***

To name some things, visible and invisible (a sculpture may be invisible): a block of
wood; a person; a mirror; a small book; a typewritten text; a hand; an arm; a head
('A head … became an object completely unknown and without dimensions' said
Alberto Giacometti); paint on cloth; paint on paper; a ladder; a large blue box; a
five person ensemble, the relations between them; a goldfish; a look; a walk; a bar;
people at a bar; a picture of a hat, a picture of a shoe, a picture of a head, etc.; a
splash of colour; a piece of plasterboard; a piece of cake; a real jug; a more or less
unusable jug, being a sculpture of a jug; a big book; a piece of furniture; a thing
made to look like a piece of furniture; a shoe, a hat, a piece of shaped metal; a
shapeless piece of clay; a stone, a sculpture of any of the foregoing familiar
materials, a sound, a silence; a piece of music; something found; words in any form
(written, spoken, shouted, printed, kept back and silently potential); a movement

(random or choreographed), a pose, assumed or struck, a gesture (random, emphatic, meaningless, imperceptible); a potato on a plate (Cézanne said: 'With an apple I shall astonish Paris,'); a scone (not of yesterday's making) against any background; the bloom on and off the plum; a conversation.

***

A thing can be any thing. So can a sculpture.

A thing, placed some where, can do some thing. A thing, placed some where cannot do nothing. Intent may determine some thing to be sculptural, in what way depends on what kind of thing it is, and where it is placed.

***

Making sculpture is not a problem; all it requires is intent. Placing sculpture some where is a problem. Where? When? Why? Whether it is good or not is a matter of history not of taste.

The why is the question that may be answered by any one who encounters the thing where it is placed. The thing might be any thing (see the arbitrary list above, remembering that there are an infinity of other things existent, potential, possible). Any thing might replace anything else.

Who places some thing some where? Any one who is a sculptor.

Any one is a sculptor. Any one is a sculpture. Any where. Any time.

Bruce McLean is a sculptor. Bruce McLean has been a sculptor for a long time, in many places. Some times he has been a sculpture.

Mel Gooding

Bruce McLean

Five Decades of Sculpture

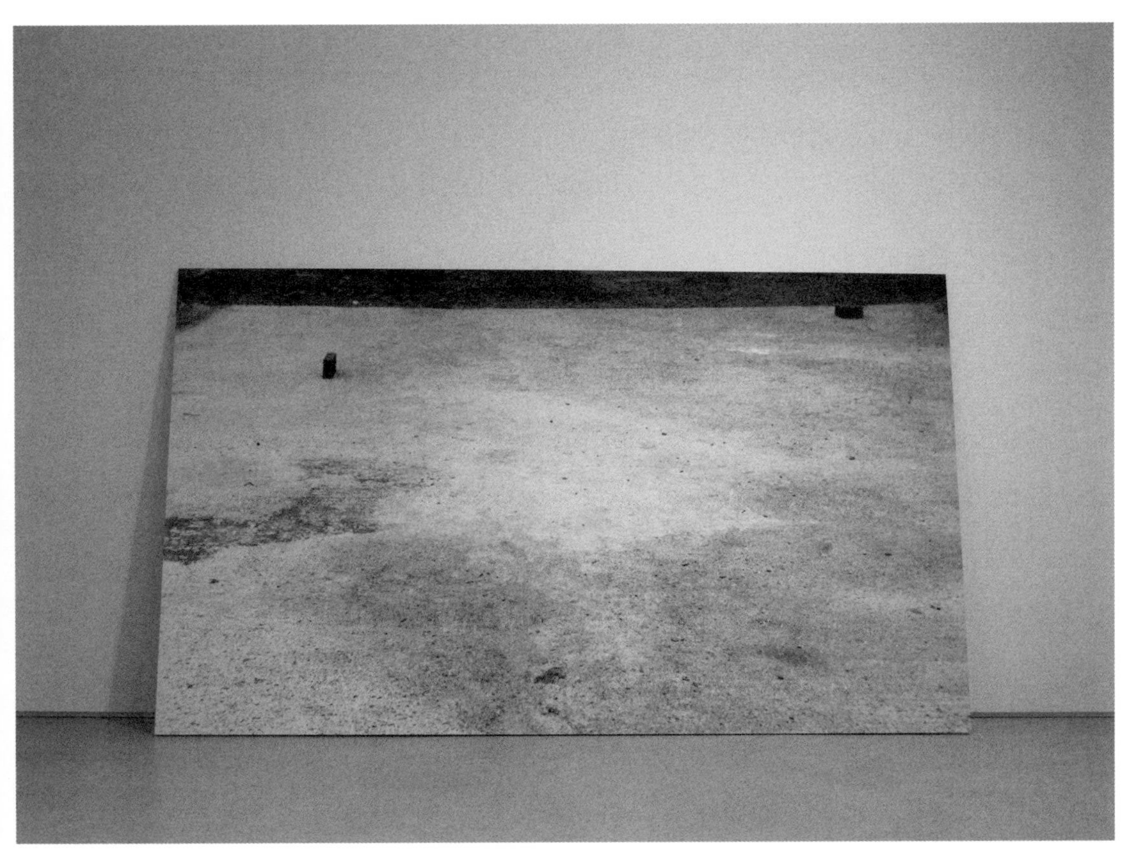

No 1:

Two part brick sculpture for concrete plinth, Stanton Road, 1967,
Re-photographed, 2018

This is a photo-documentation of a sculpture. It is not the sculpture. 52 years later I photocopied the documentation, enlarged it, and turned the photograph of the two bricks on a concrete plinth into a photo-sculpture. I then photographed the photo-sculpture, when installed in the gallery, and made another photo-sculpture of the photo-sculpture.

No 2:

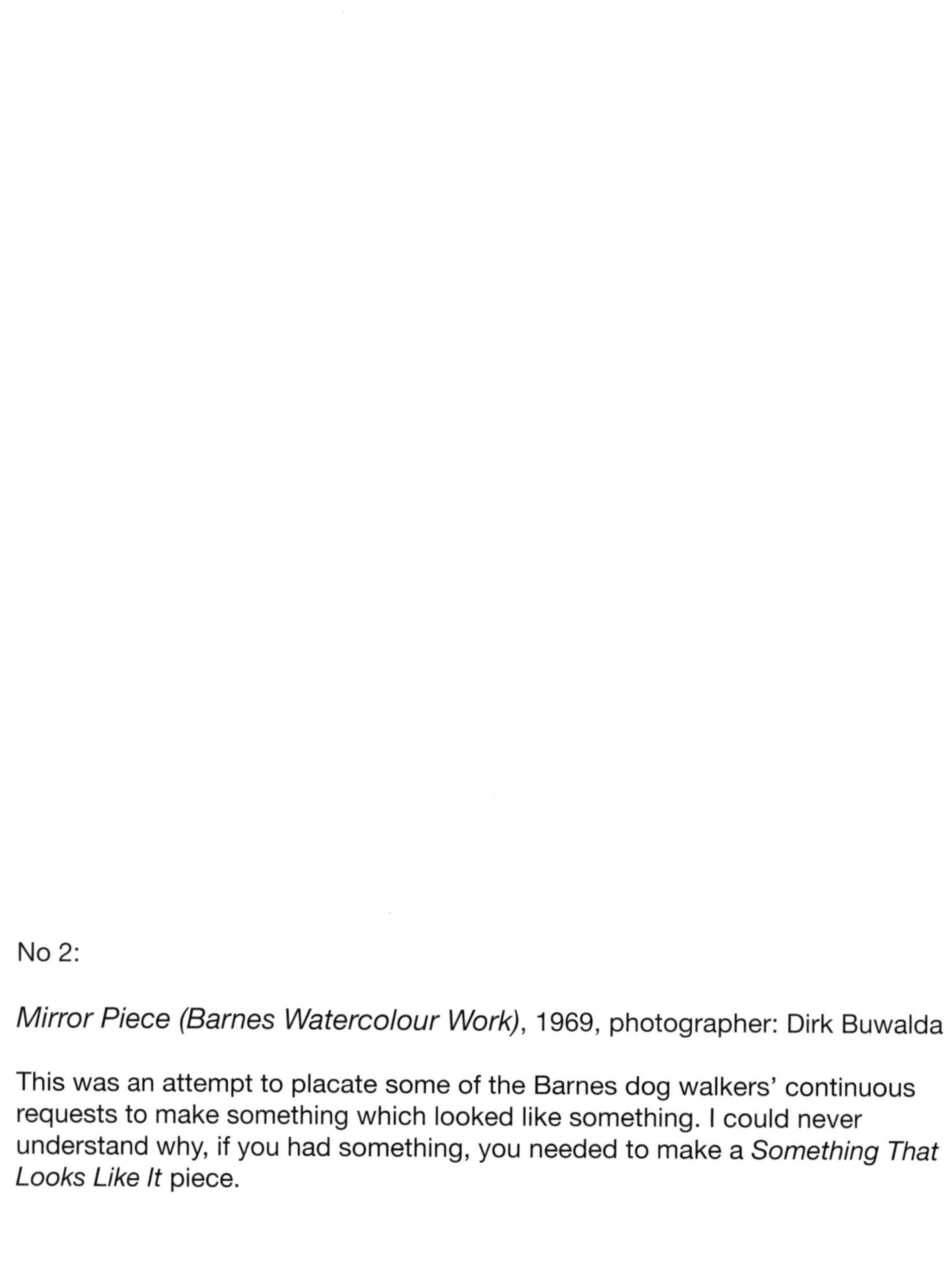

Mirror Piece (Barnes Watercolour Work), 1969, photographer: Dirk Buwalda

This was an attempt to placate some of the Barnes dog walkers' continuous requests to make something which looked like something. I could never understand why, if you had something, you needed to make a *Something That Looks Like It* piece.

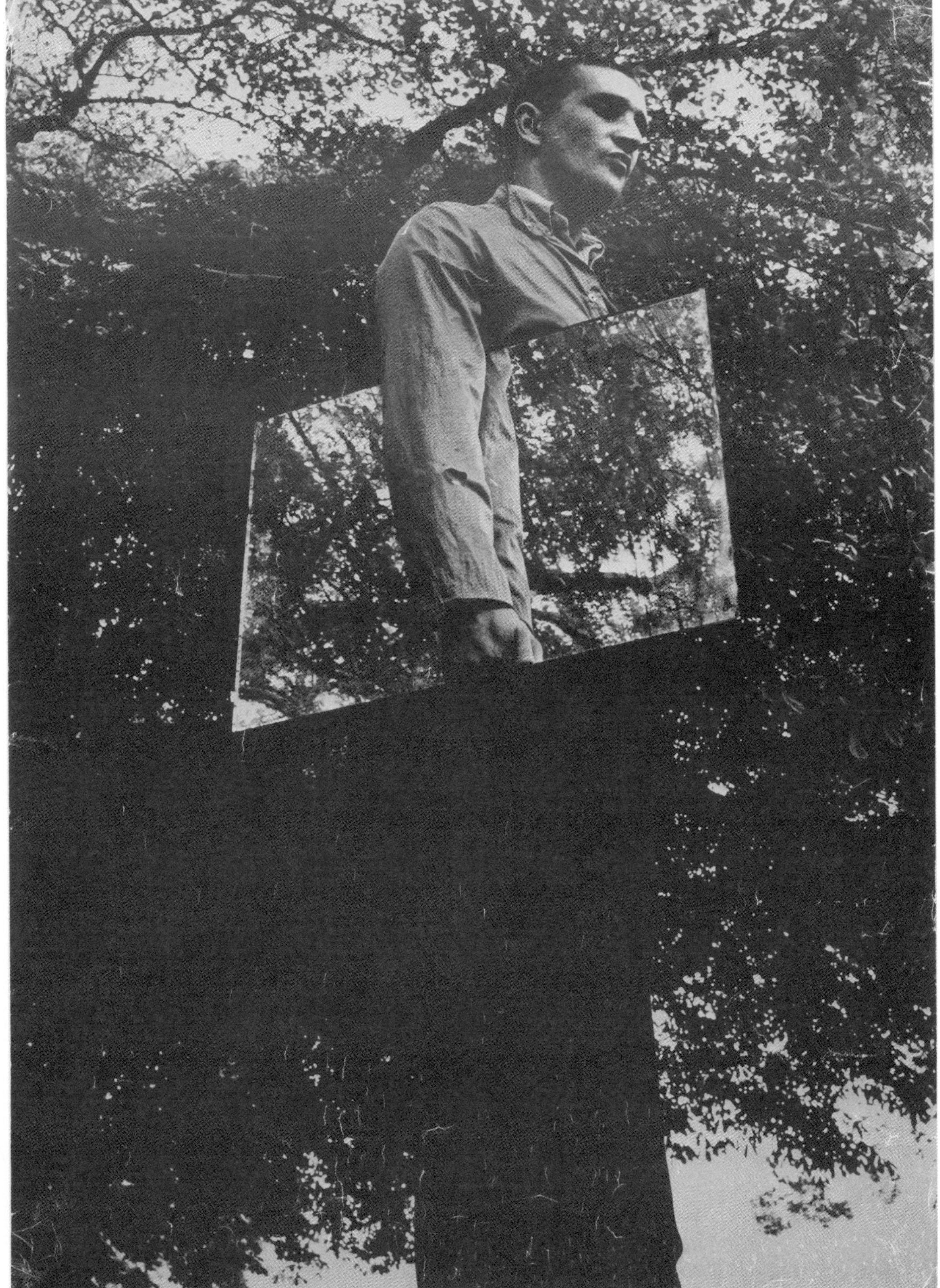

No 3:

Fallen Warrior, 1969, photographer: Dirk Buwalda

This is one of only a few works of mine which reference Henry Moore, and
precedes *Pose Work for Plinths,* 1971 by 2 years. This work was made as a
photo work and was not documentation of a live action sculpture! I believe
that it is a more interesting work than *Pose Work for Plinths* as the metal
helmet is World War One, the boots Doc Martin. Ding Dong was only said once
by Leslie Philips in the Carry On films... Same problem.

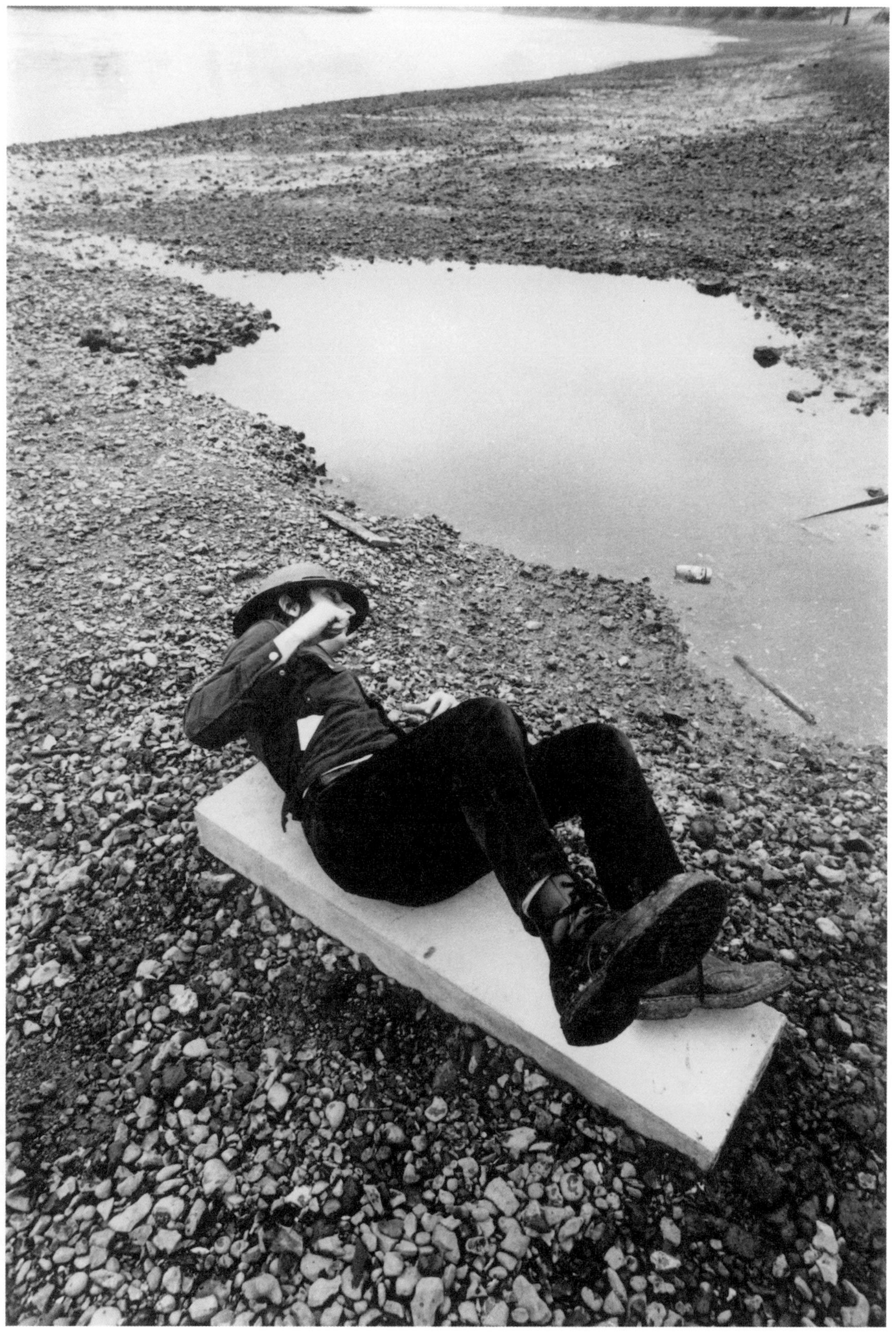

No 4:

King for a day, 1969, presented Tate Gallery, Millbank, 11th March 1972,
photographer: Dirk Buwalda

This particular work came about after an evening going to Charles Harrison's art
party in Belsize Park. I was with Rosy, Lucy Lippard, and Seth Zieglaub. When we
arrived at the party, which was quite empty, but for a few dreary second division
conceptual artists whinging in a corner, Seth said to me, 'is this the hottest ticket
in town?', 'it looks like it to me', I replied. So, we decided to have a drink, take a
bottle of vodka, and leave the party immediately.

That night, on my way home I decided to stop being an artist. I had heard that if
you have a retrospective at the Tate, that's the end of your life as an artist, so the
obvious thing to do was to create a retrospective. I thereby proceeded to write
a thousand pieces for my retrospective catalogue, which I thought could be the
show, as well as the catalogue of the show. I would exhibit the catalogues on the
floor, not on a plinth. Visitors would come, buy a catalogue, take it away, and the
show would gradually and slowly disappear, and I with it.

Catalogued, documented, and put on the shelf or the plinth. Probably not the floor
again.

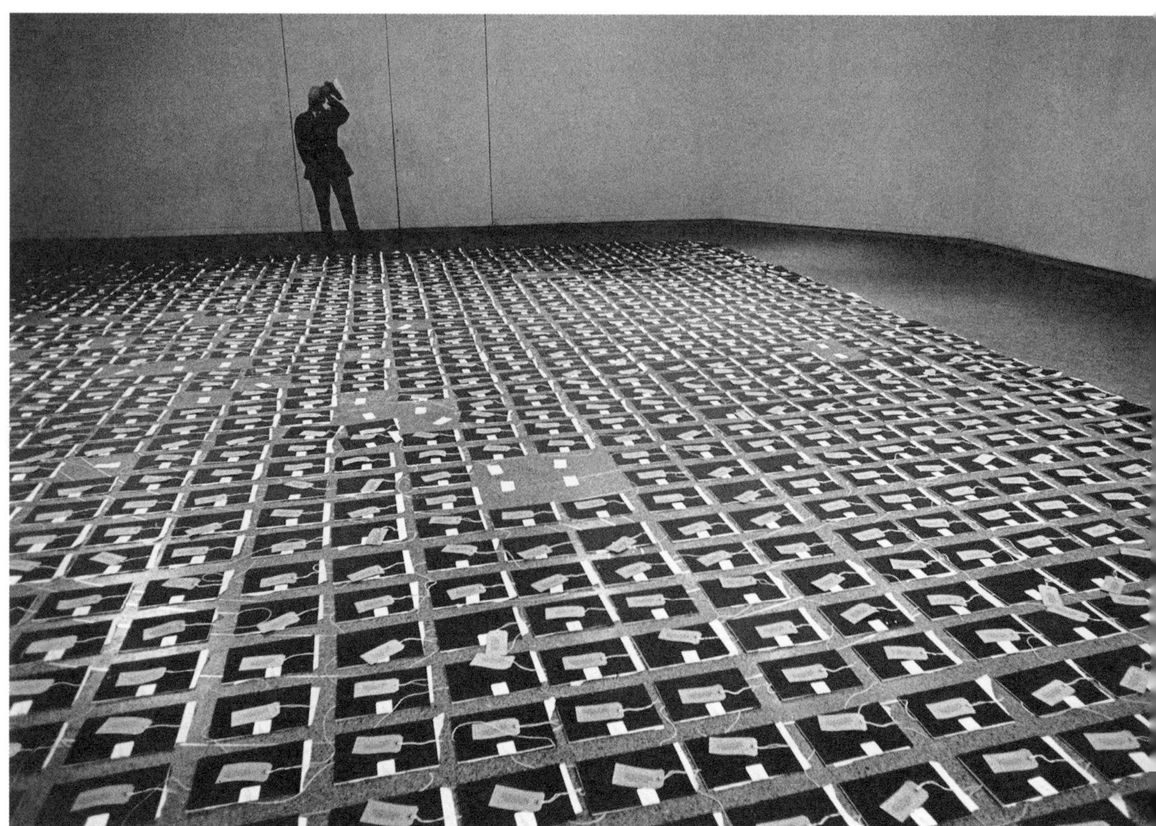

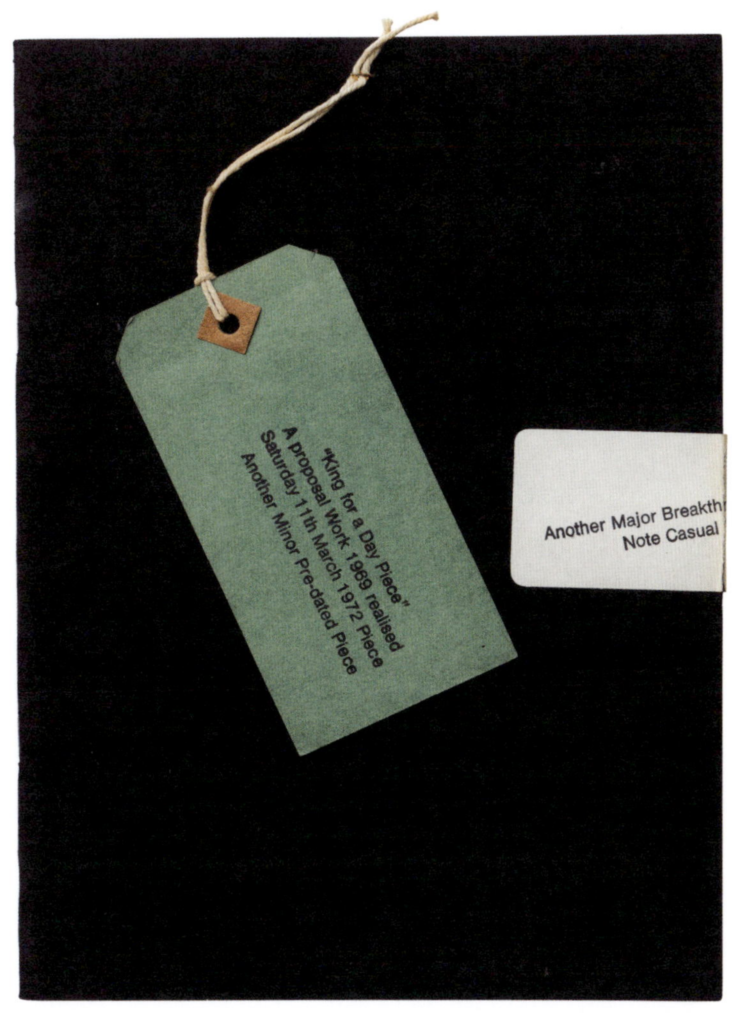

No 4a:

King for a Day and 999 other pieces / works / things etc. 1969, London:
Situation Publications, 1972

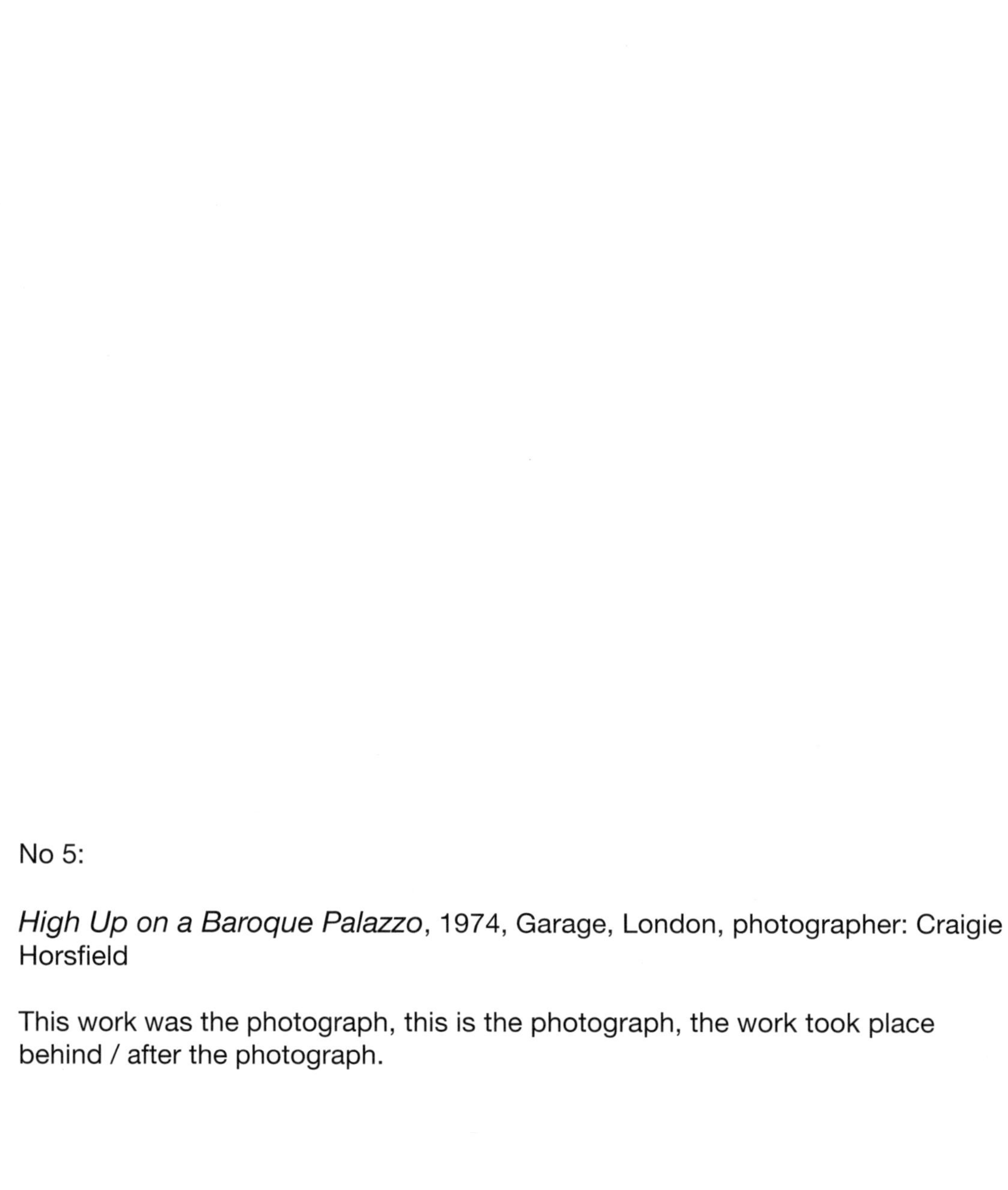

No 5:

High Up on a Baroque Palazzo, 1974, Garage, London, photographer: Craigie
Horsfield

This work was the photograph, this is the photograph, the work took place
behind / after the photograph.

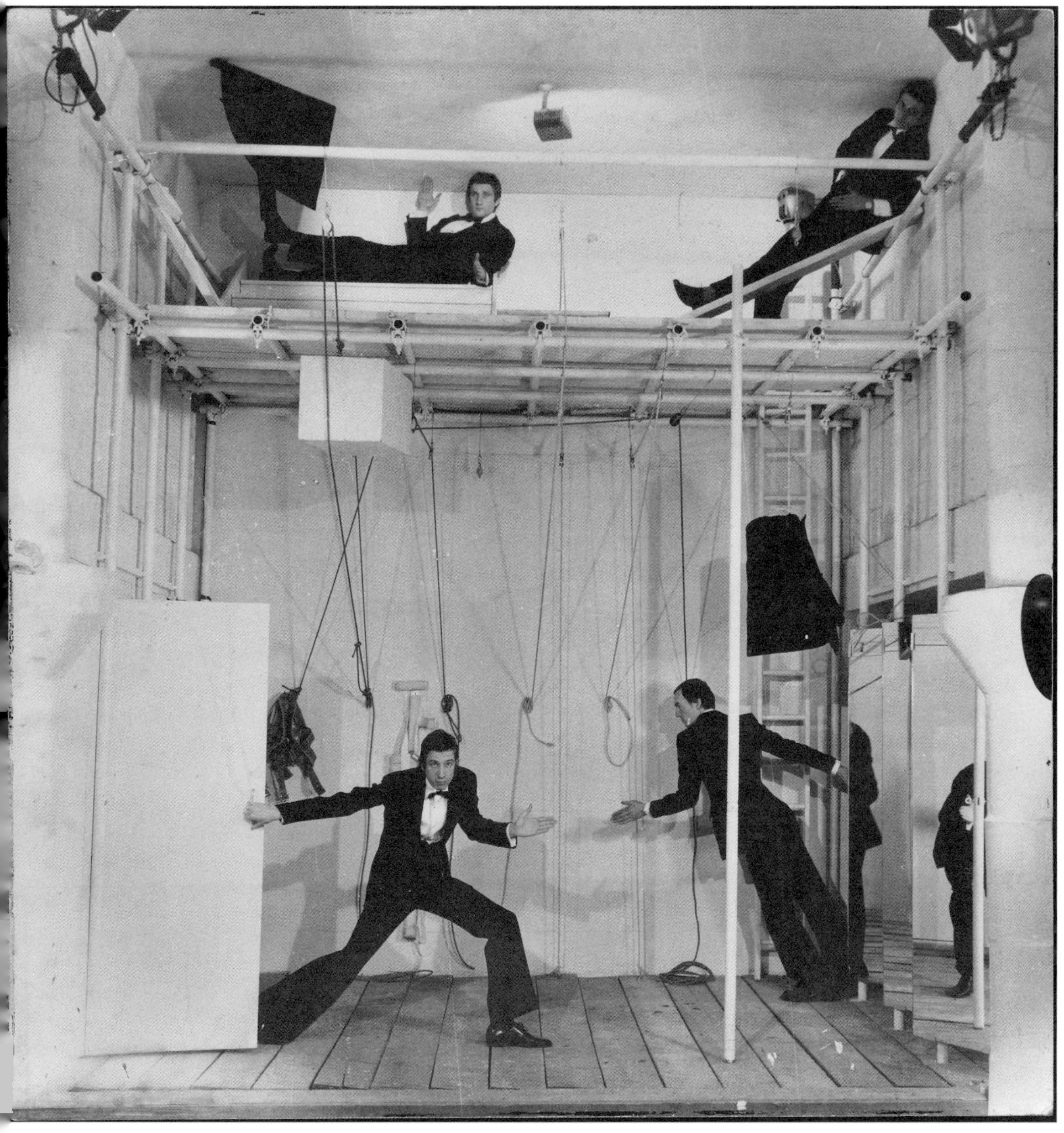

No 6:

Chinese balancing act against a red background, 1977, screenprint,
76.2 x 92.5 cms

This was a very influential work: minimal, focused, and political.

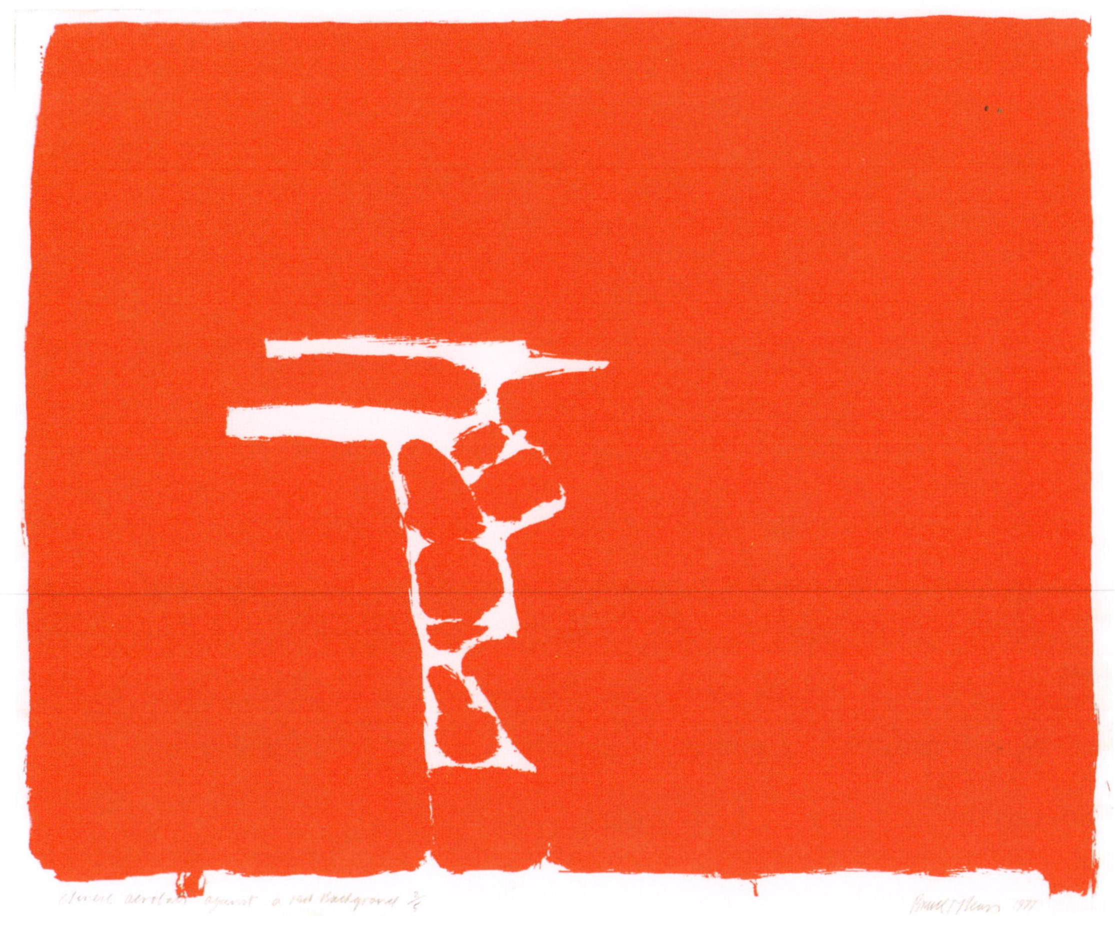
Christ abstract against a red background 2/4
Bruce McLean 1977

No 7:

A Certain Smile, 1978, acrylic and crayon on paper, 110.5 x 135.2 cms

Early coloured drawing, articulating a projected live work.

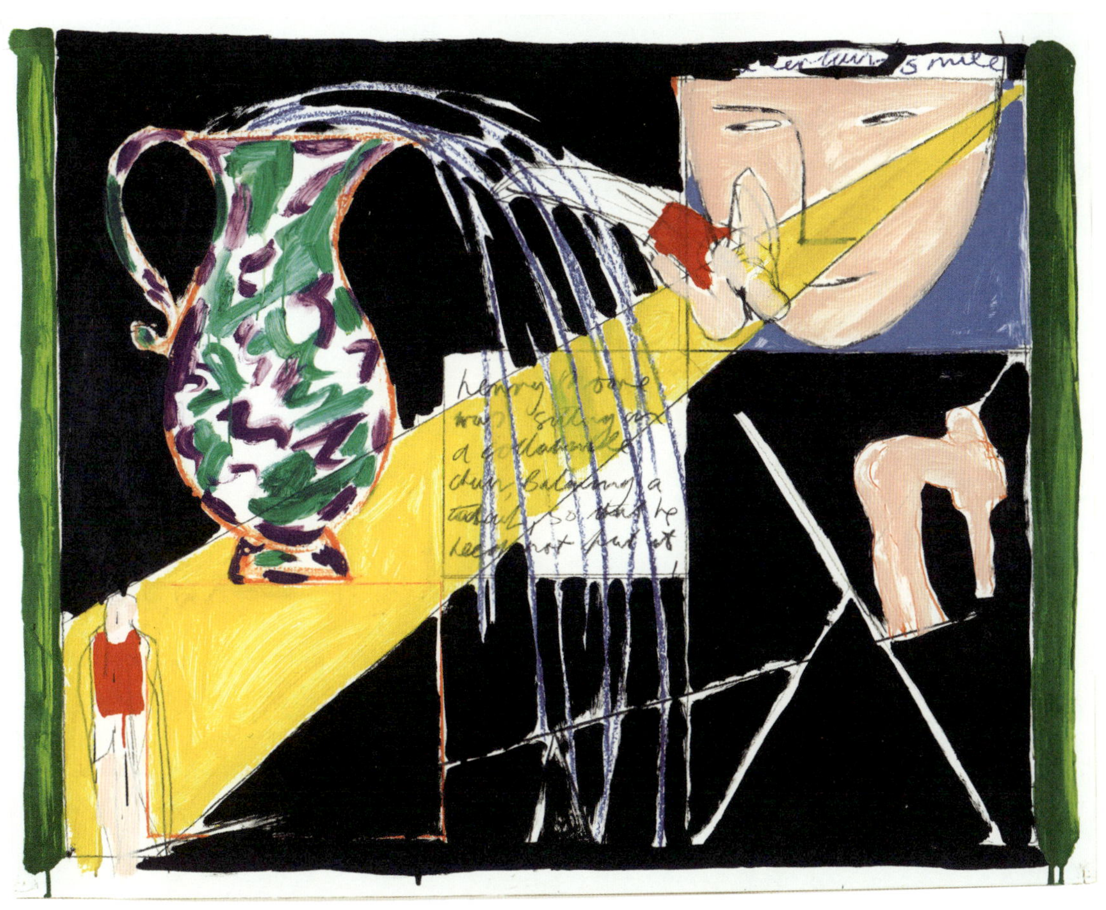
smile

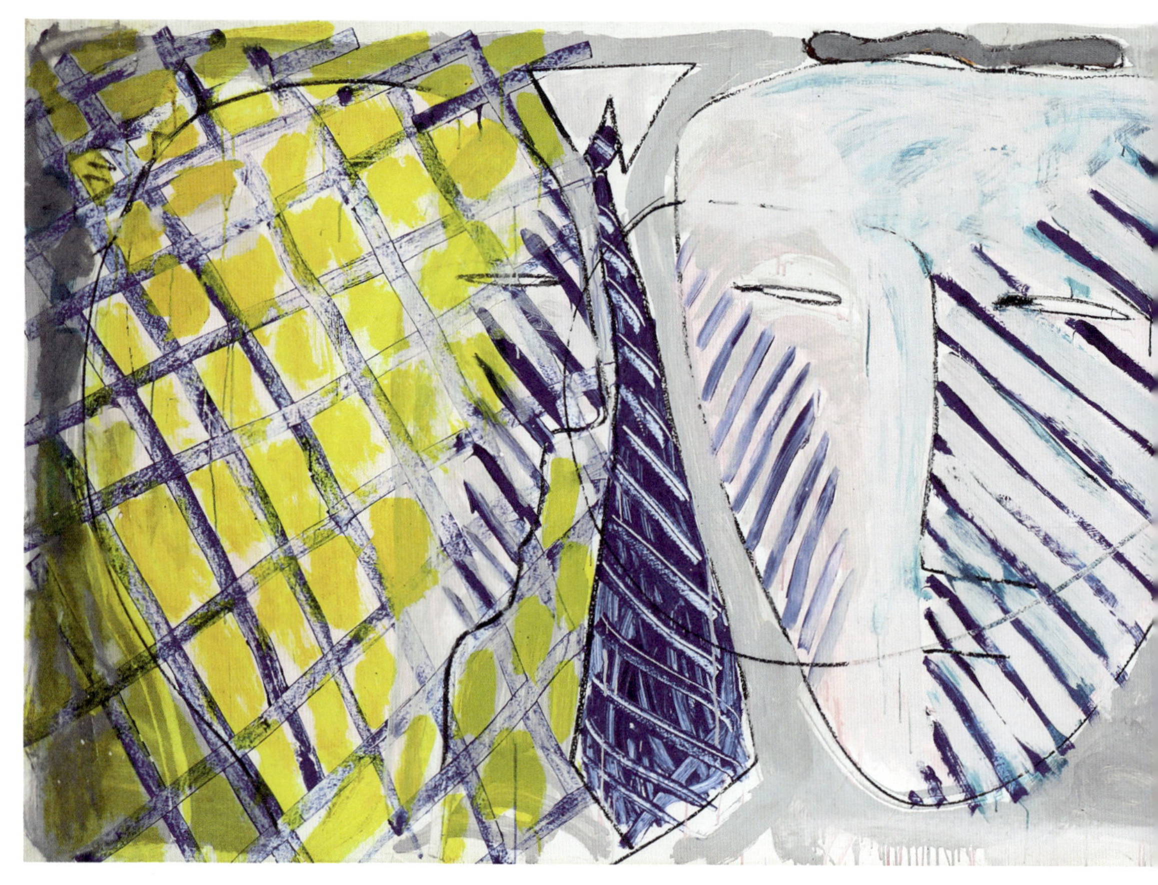

No 8:

The ties, the looks, 1980, acrylic on paper mounted on canvas, 137 x 387 cms

Striped new ties and old ties.

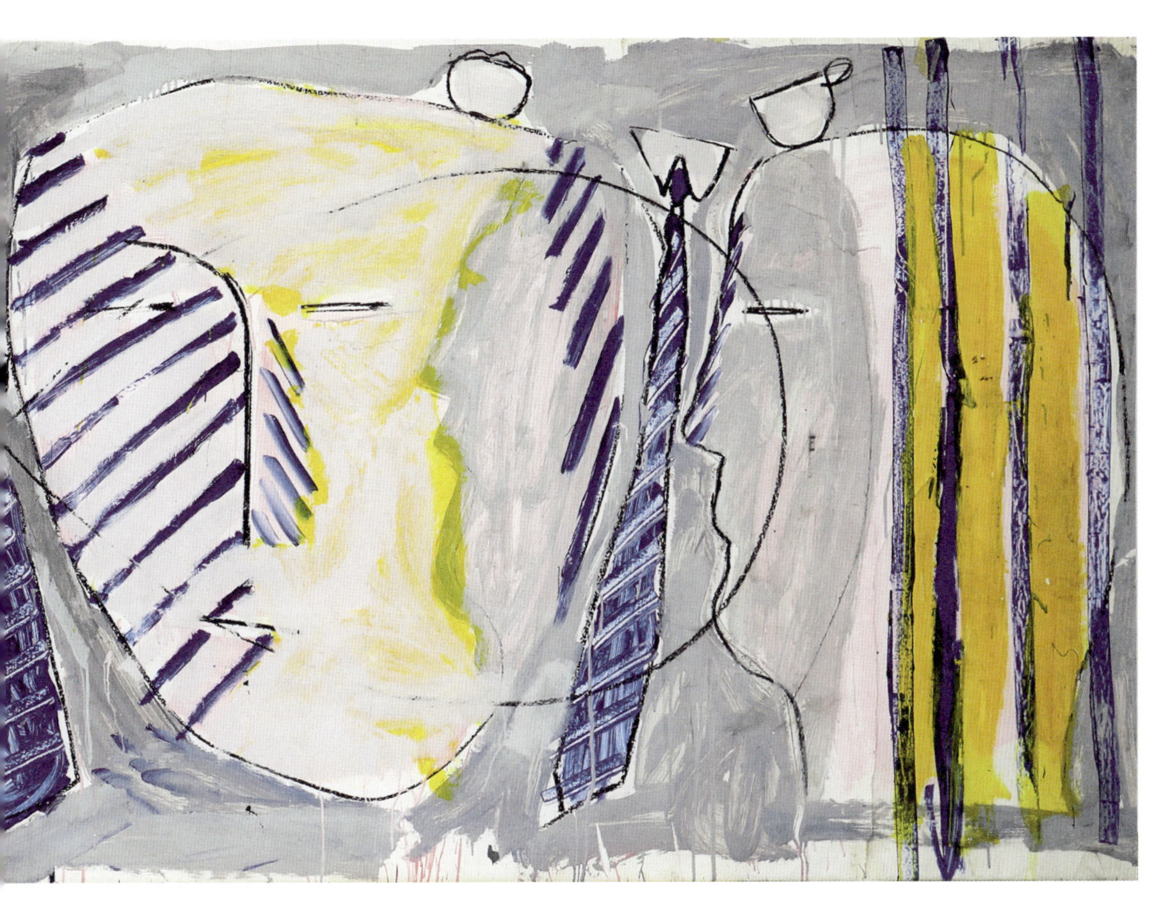

No 9:

Oriental Garden Kyoto, 1982, acrylic on cotton duck, 250 x 350 cms, Walker Art Gallery, Liverpool

This painting is (intentionally) the same size as the gardens I observed in Kyoto.

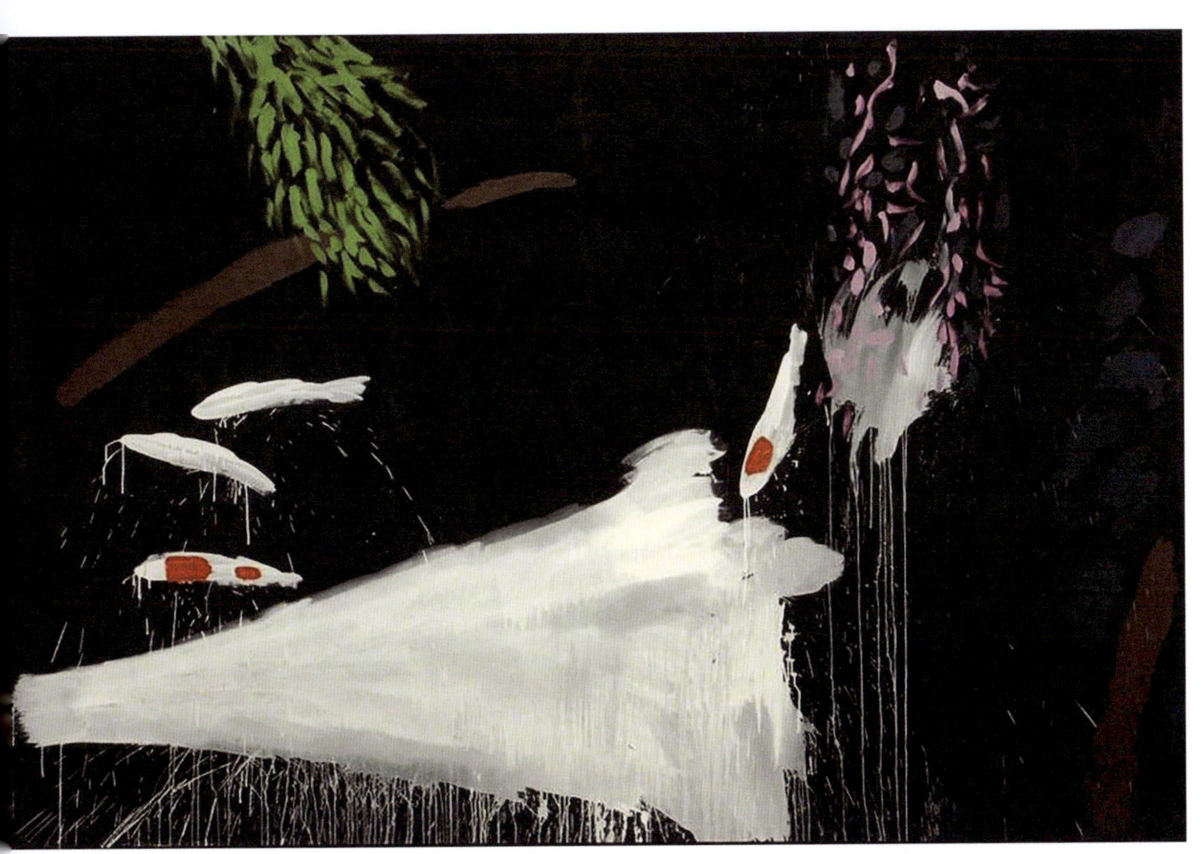

No 10:

Yet Another Bad Turn Up, text for tape, 1983

Yet another bad turn up
a work based on a trouser
cut in the documenta 7 area
which table hi there, mmmm
oh ho well leave the beer
beige I think with some flare
coming in on the right zeit
moving up street feet
that sort of bad turn up
again for the book, no what
I mean.
yet another bad turn up
taken the advice to base
on actually scene trouser
cut/dash in the documenta
area, which table on no bad move
coming in on the right zeit
that sort of bad turn up
again for the book, know what I mean
beige I believe with a moderate to
sixties flare oh no
bad one billo/brillo
who makes the decisions
based on the style dilemma in the
selecter, matching beige
chas and dave
kevin and trace
common as much
flash as fuck
bad lapel
bad move
bad decision
bad one brillo
beige courtelle stretch flares
tight round the bum
hugging the knee and
flared at the ankle
the foremost exponent of
media control looses in the
trouser stakes
the whole operation revealed in a badly cut
pair of rather nasty trouser.
The work dares to ask questions about decisions
The great courtelle trouser crisis.

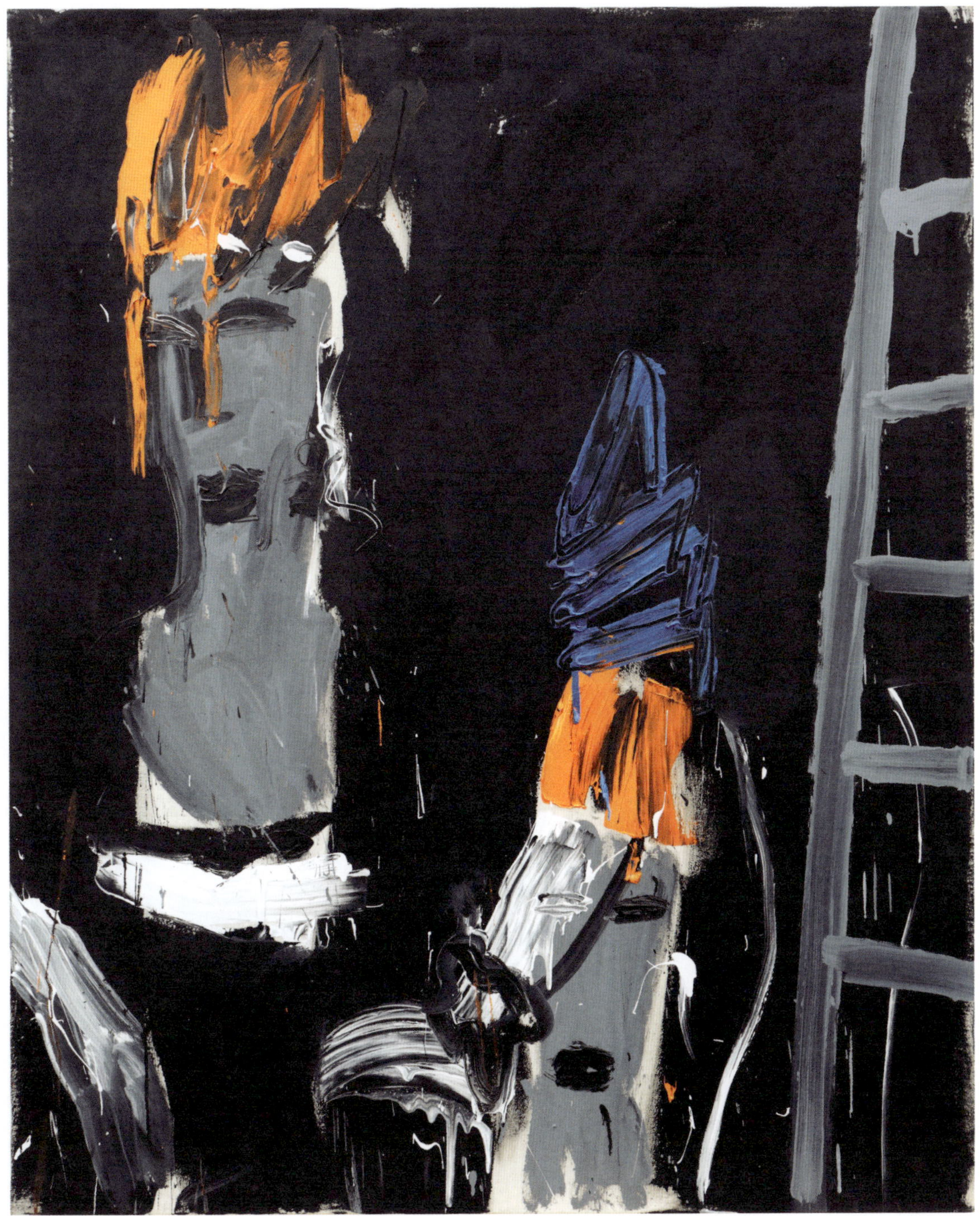

No 11:

Gucci Shoe Heads, 1983, oil and acrylic on canvas, 213 x 167 cms

Shoe heads, relating to the African practice of placing possessions on your head. Moving and continuously changing sculptures.

No 12:

Fireplace sculpture, 1987, mild steel, 240 x 294 x 82 cms

A place for a lean… Referencing Robert Adams and Anthony Caro.
Tall people to the left, short people to the right. A perfect mantle piece.

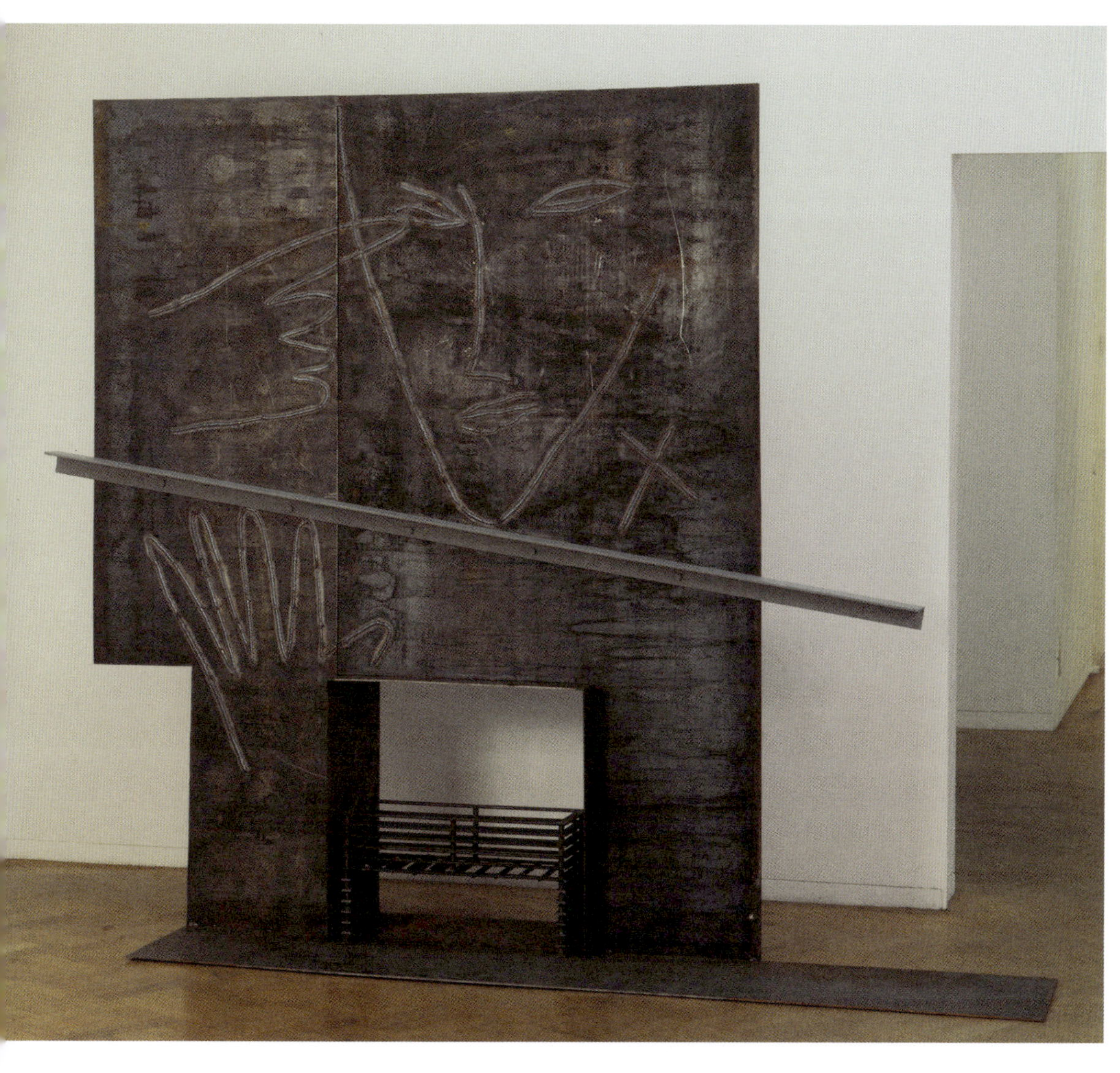

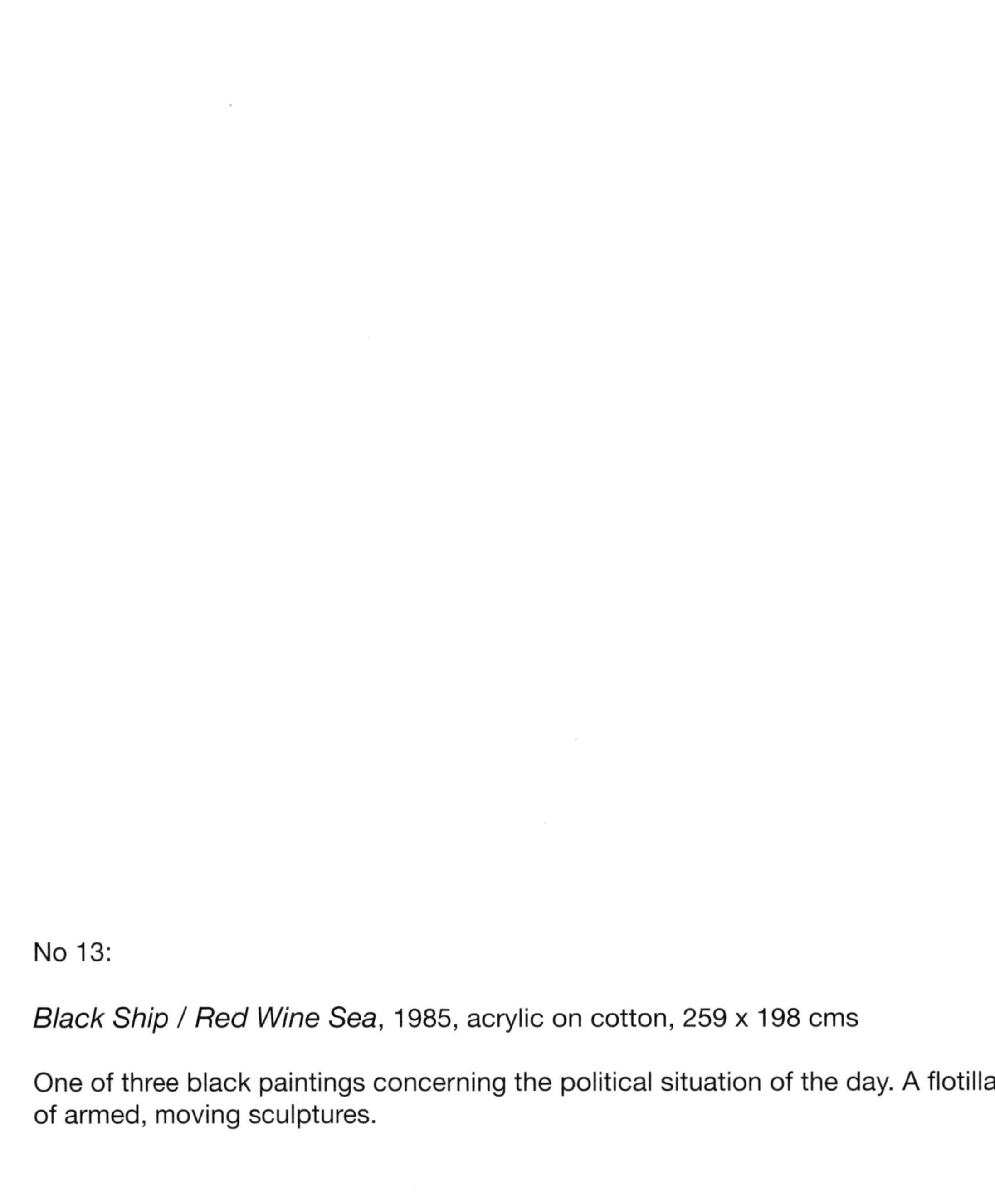

No 13:

Black Ship / Red Wine Sea, 1985, acrylic on cotton, 259 x 198 cms

One of three black paintings concerning the political situation of the day. A flotilla of armed, moving sculptures.

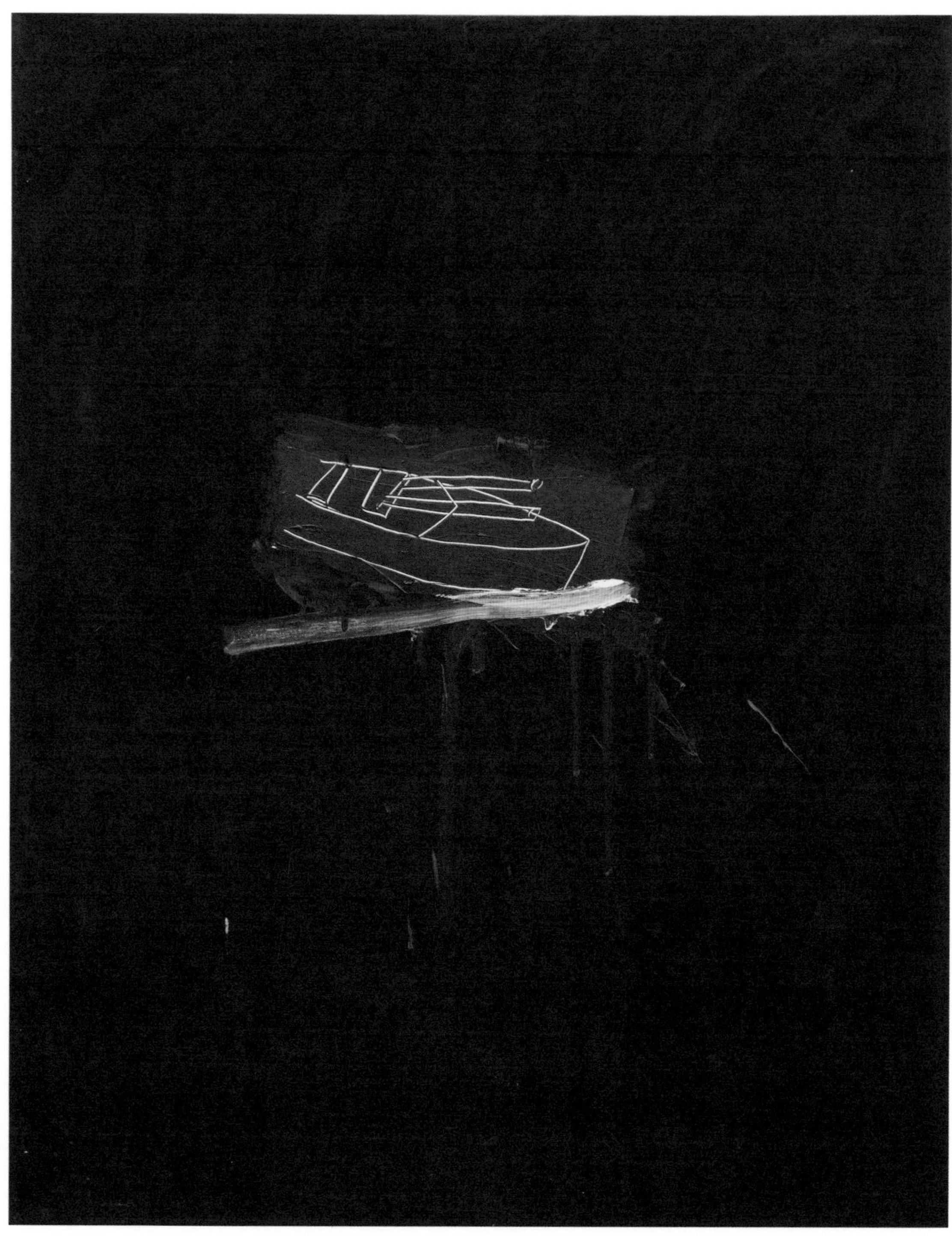

No 14:

Splash Painting, 1986, oil, acrylic and collage on canvas, 282 x 200 cms

Pouring, throwing wasting. Excess work dealing with the subject of excess.

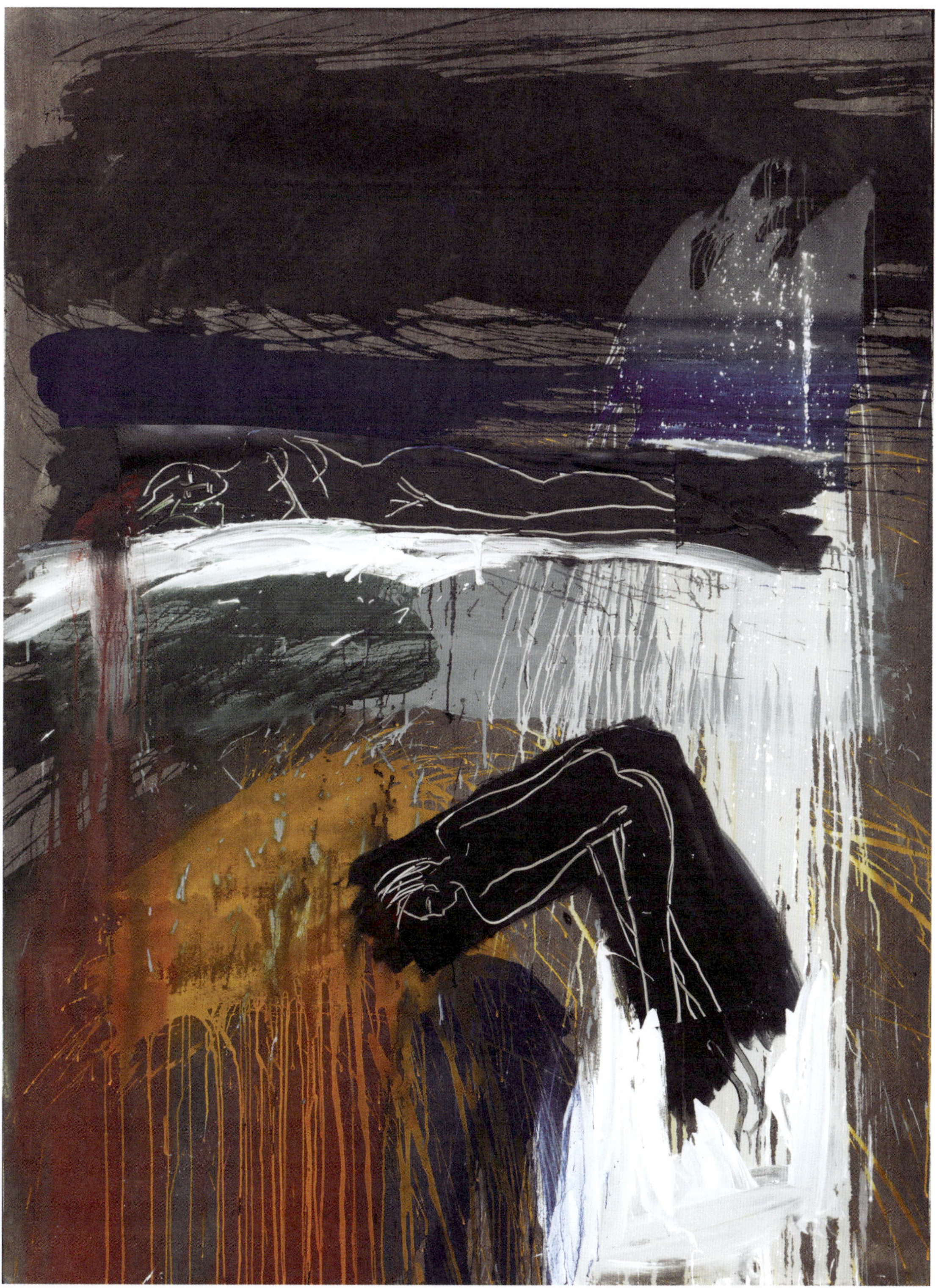

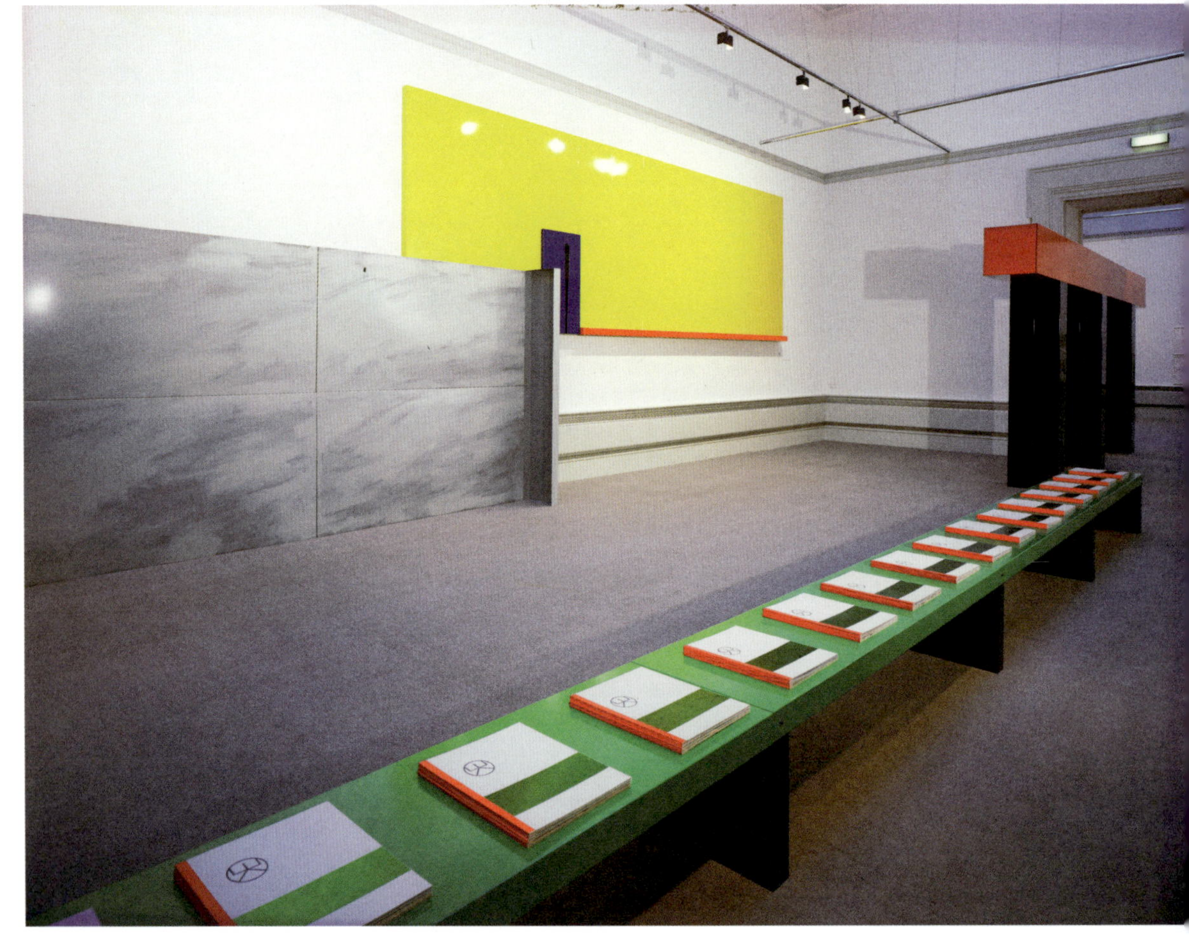

No 15:

A table sculpture for books, 1991, metal

Installation shot of grey sculpture for standing in and walking around, a
yellow painting not to focus on with blue and red attachments and a red and black
bridge sculpture.

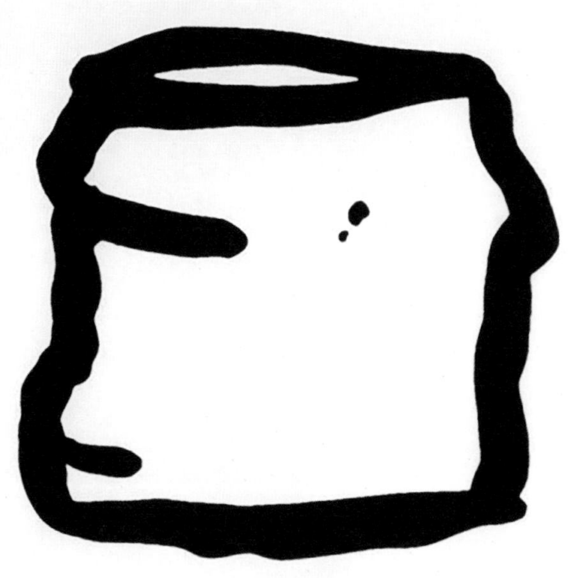

No 16:

A Scone in a White Interior, from *a Scone off a Plate*, a Knife Edge Book, 1990

A book dealing with the positioning of scones / stones / sculptors /
sculptures in relation to plinths, plates etc.

No 17:

Jaffa, Jaffa, Jaffa, 1991, lacquer paint and enamel on steel panel, with attached red sculpture, 208.5 x 416 x 22.2 cms, Museum Moderner Kunst, Stiftung Ludwig, Wein.

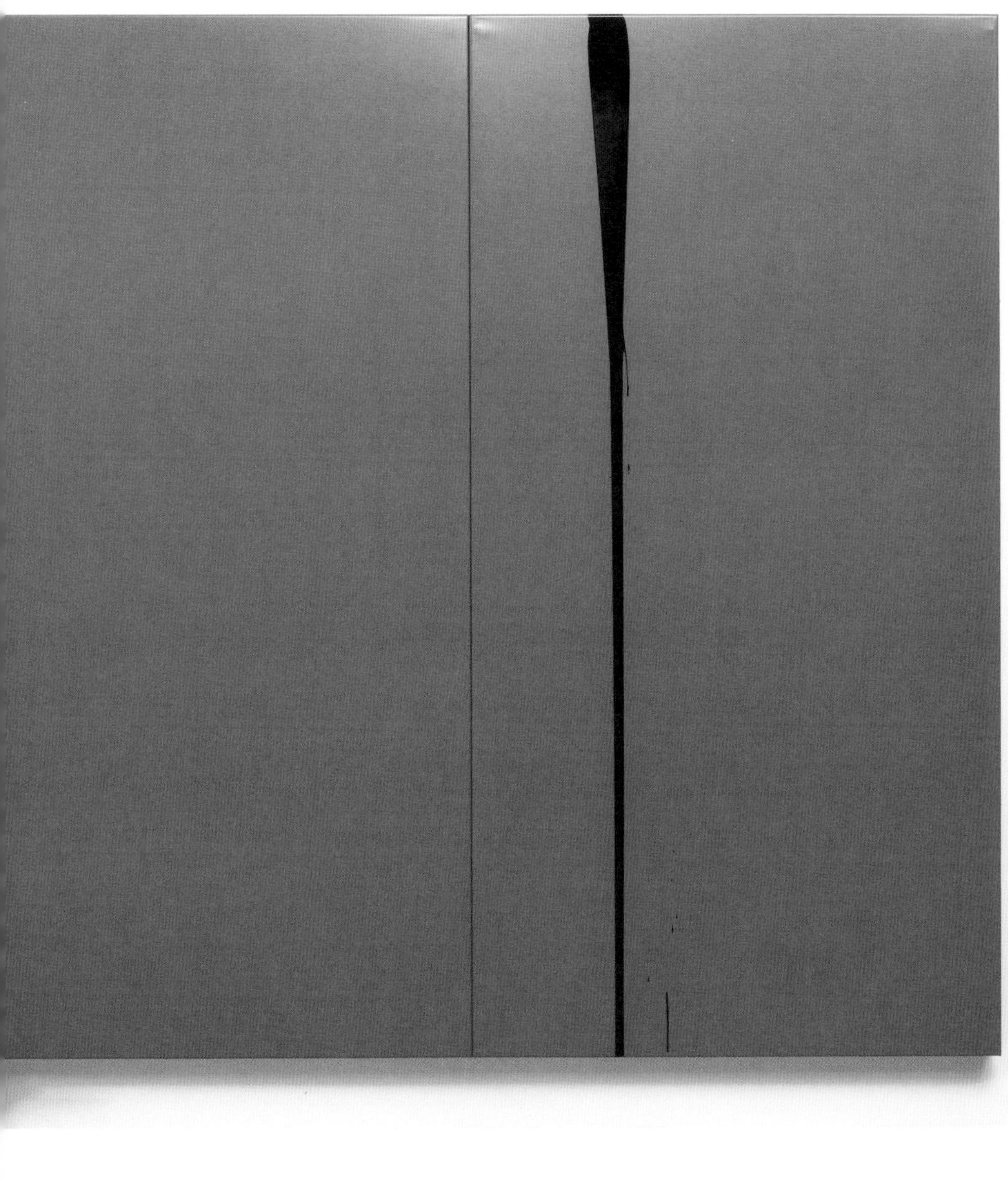

No 18:

Argyle Street Project Poster, 1994

A poster to encourage perambulating, prancing, pirouetting, positioning, posing, placing, and parading.

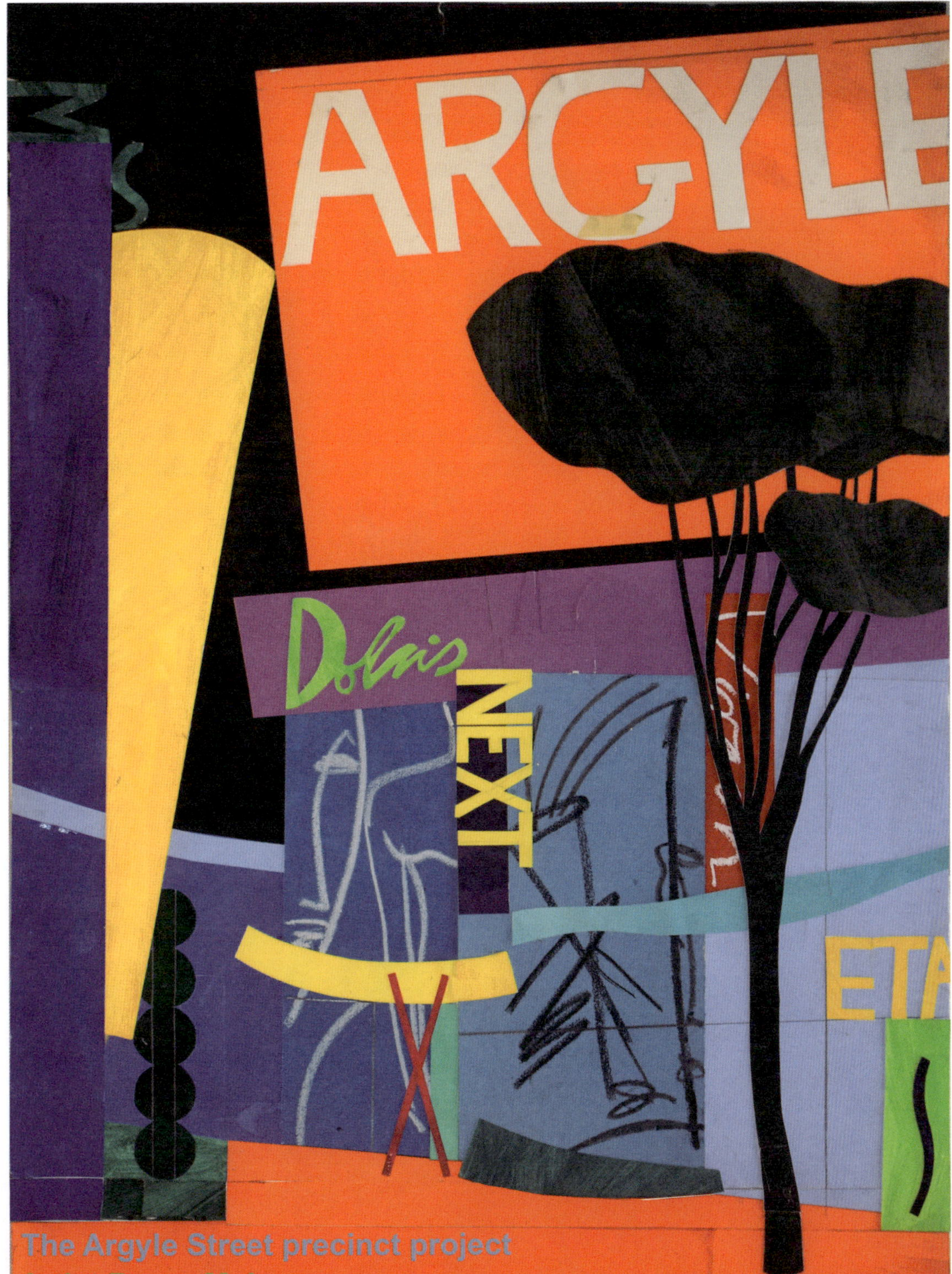

The Argyle Street precinct project
Artist Bruce McLean has been invited to make a proposition for a precinct for:
performing, pointing, positioning, placing, perambulating, pirouetting, posing and parading.

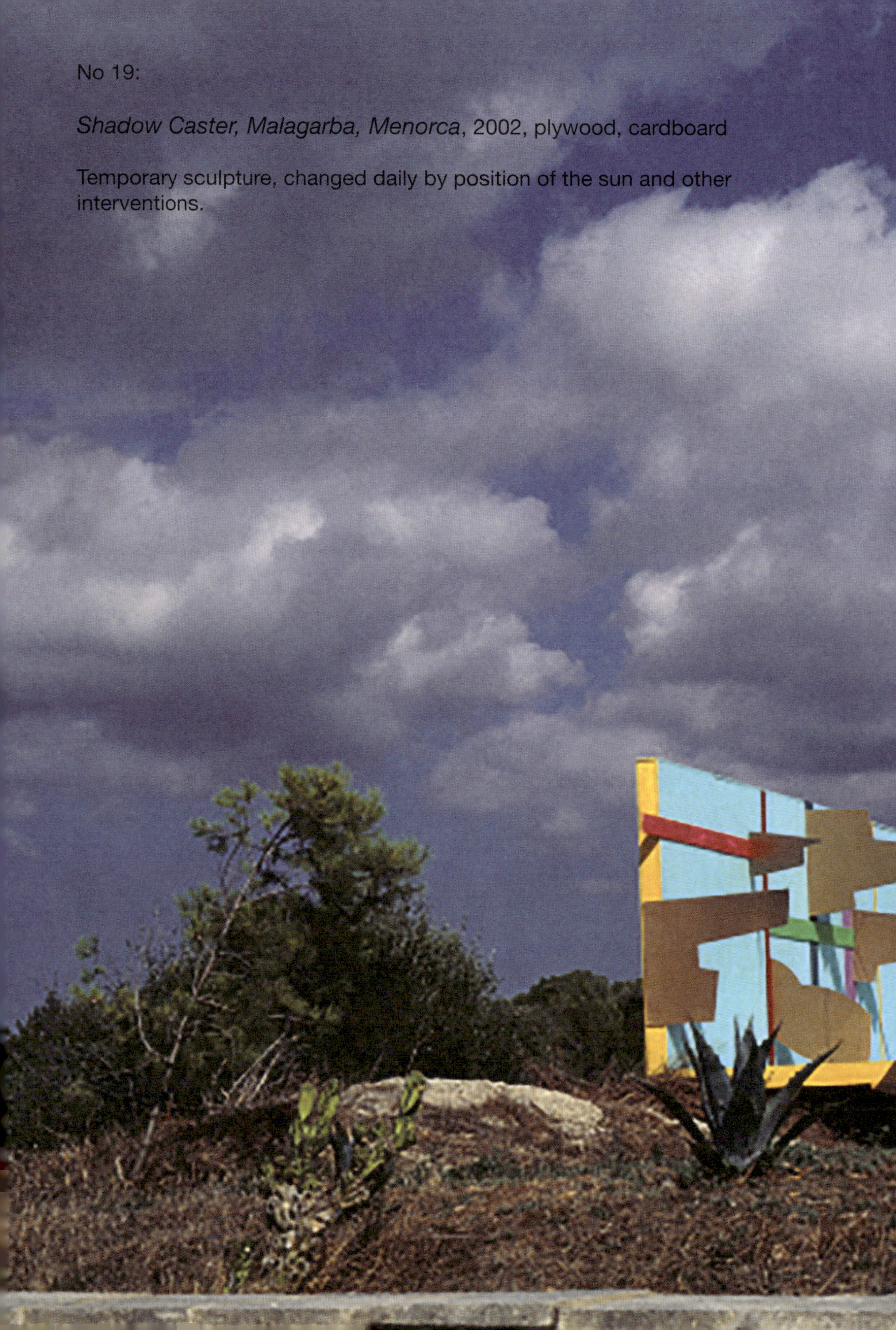

No 19:

Shadow Caster, Malagarba, Menorca, 2002, plywood, cardboard

Temporary sculpture, changed daily by position of the sun and other interventions.

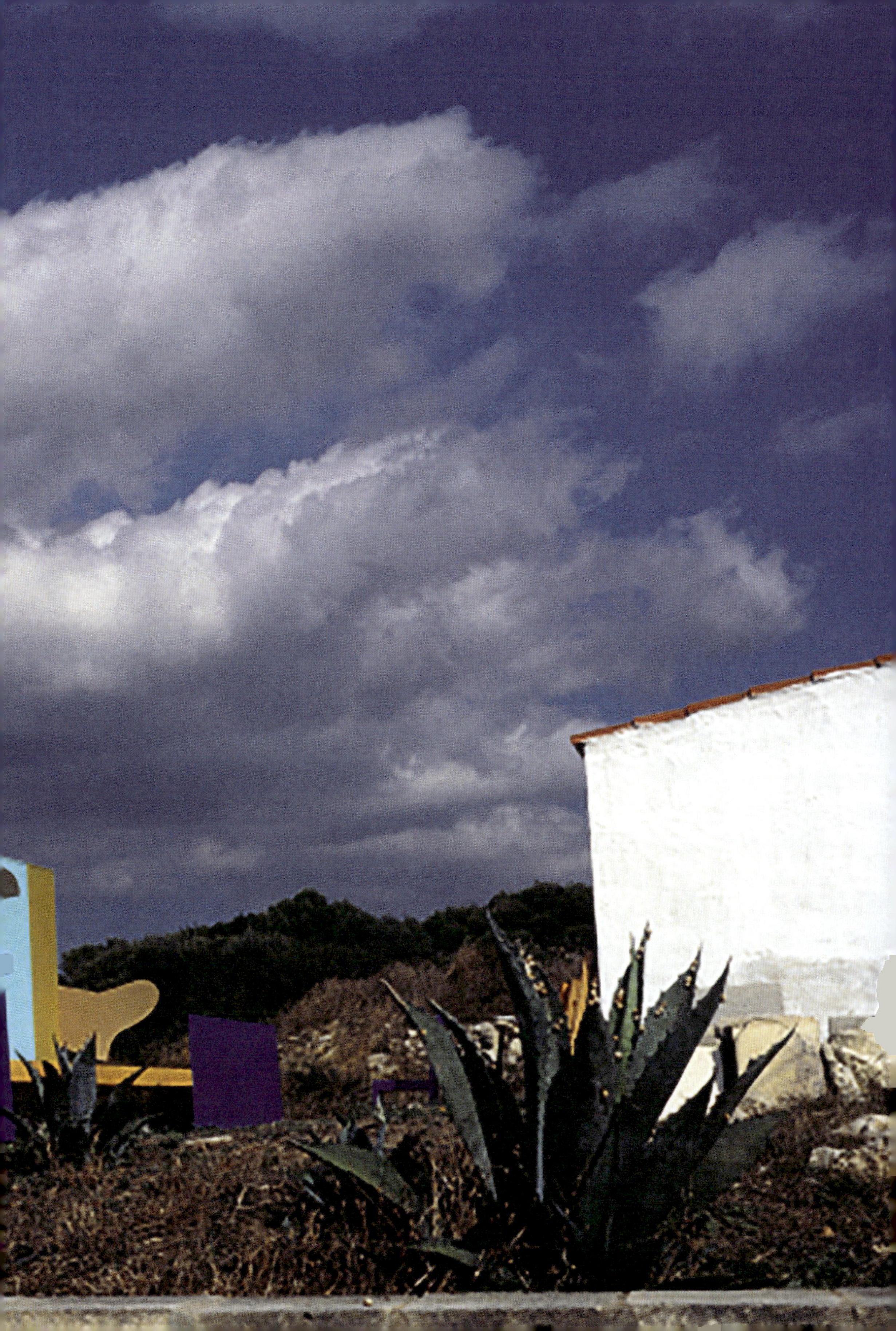

No 20:

Dark Garden with Constructed Shadow, 2009, acrylic and oil on canvas,
225 x 200 cms

Grey garden painting referencing sculpture garden (not sculpture park).

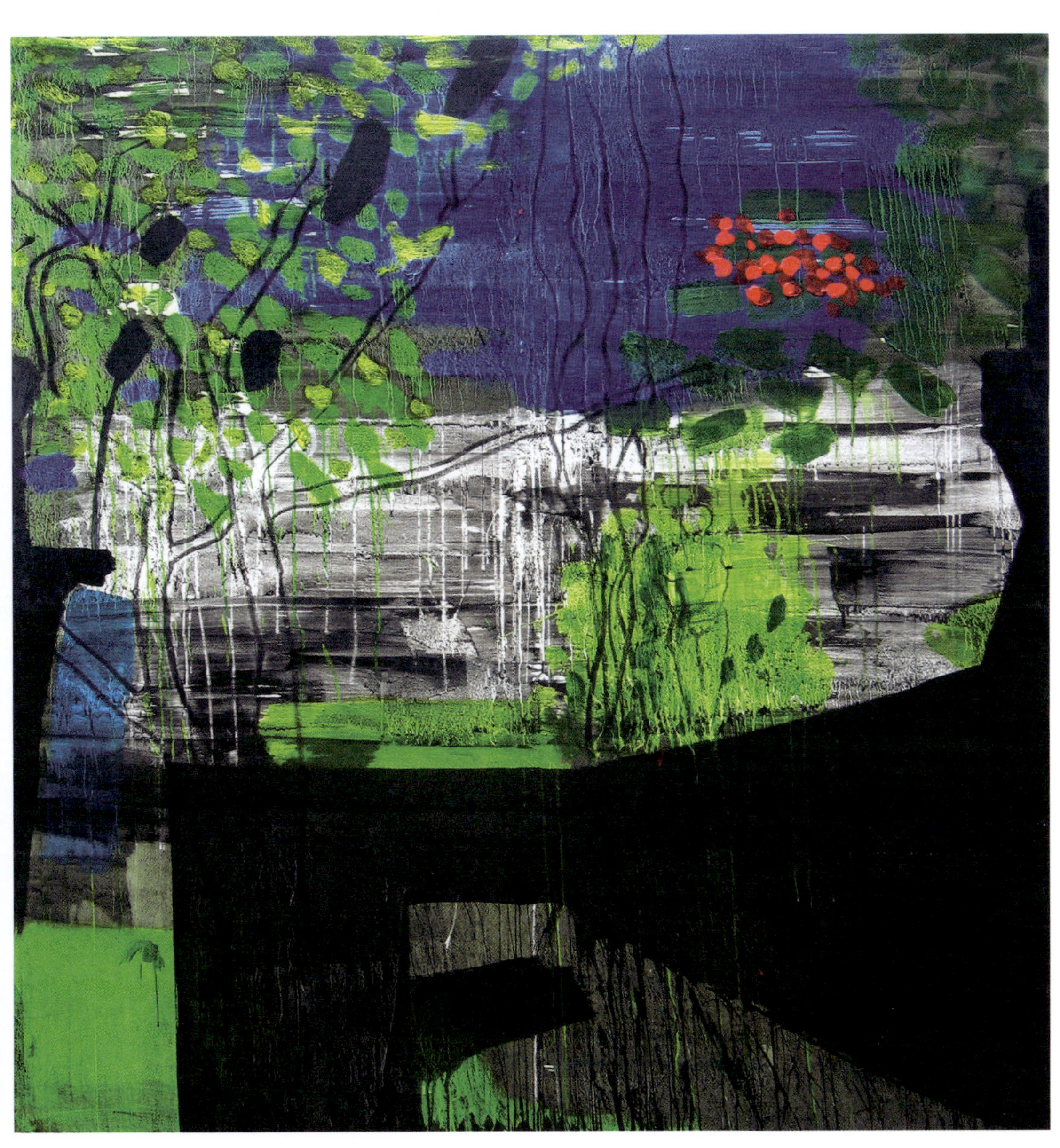

No 21:

The Generation Game of Sculpture (a cuddly toy, no, I've already said that...), 2010, oil, acrylic and charcoal on canvas, 250 x 360 cms

Trying to remember sculptures new and old.

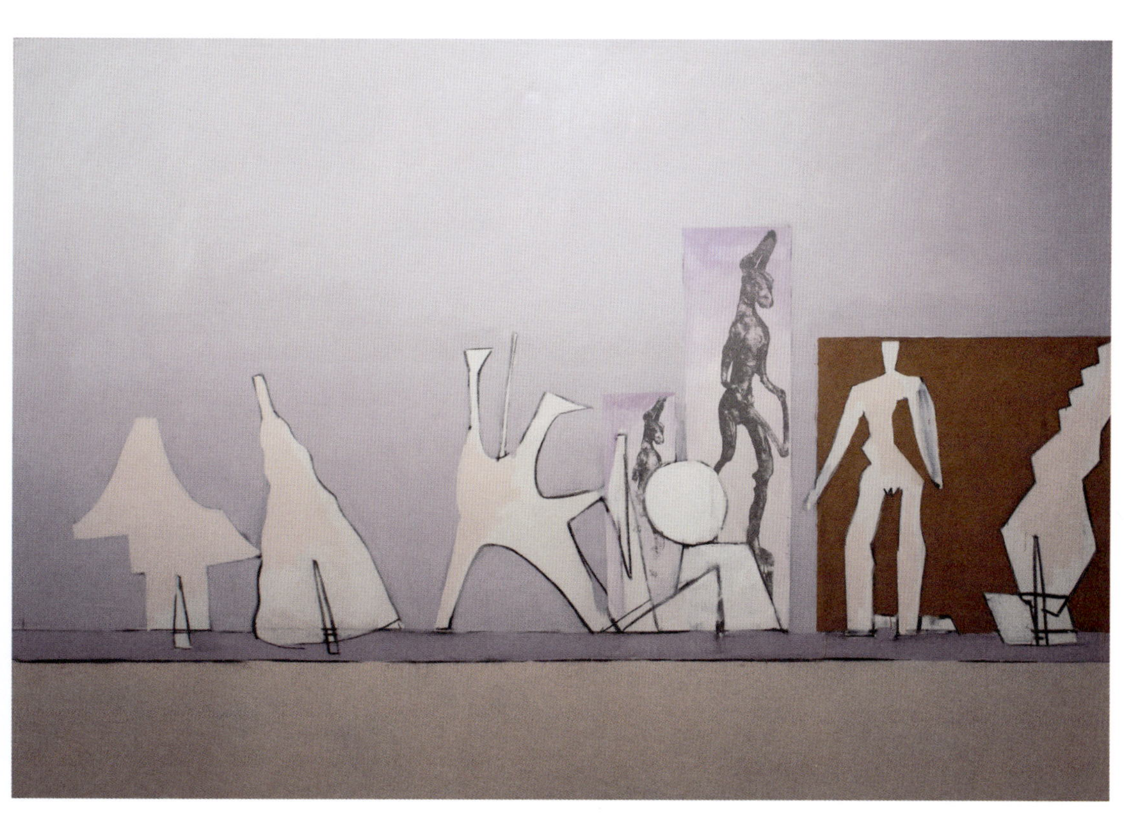

No 22:

Waiter, excuse me! There's a Bruce McLean cut-out sculpture in my soup,
2011, oil acrylic and charcoal on canvas, 225 x 200 cms

Painting constructed like a collage, using collage as a starting point relating to the
film *Waiter, Waiter,* 2010.

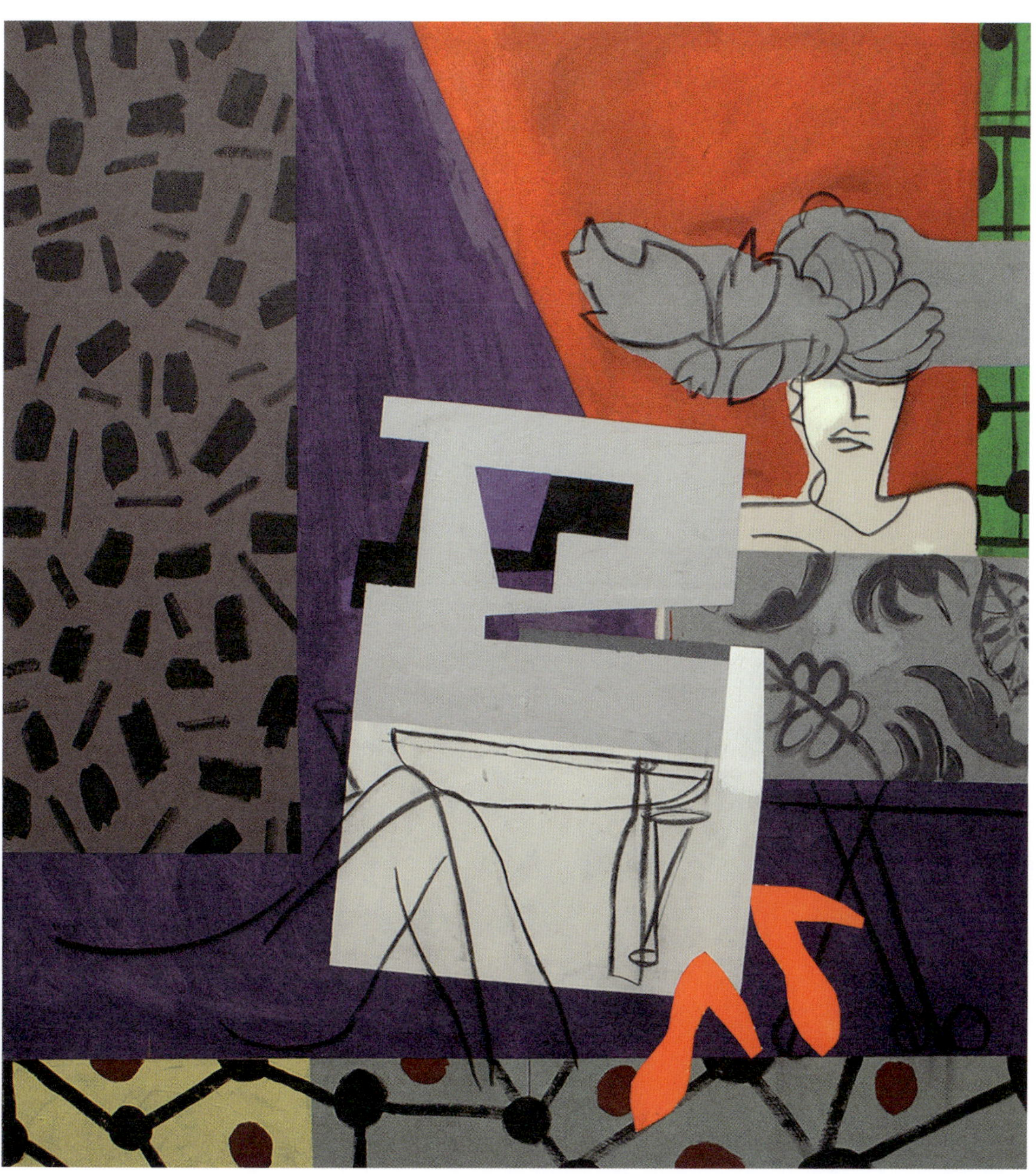

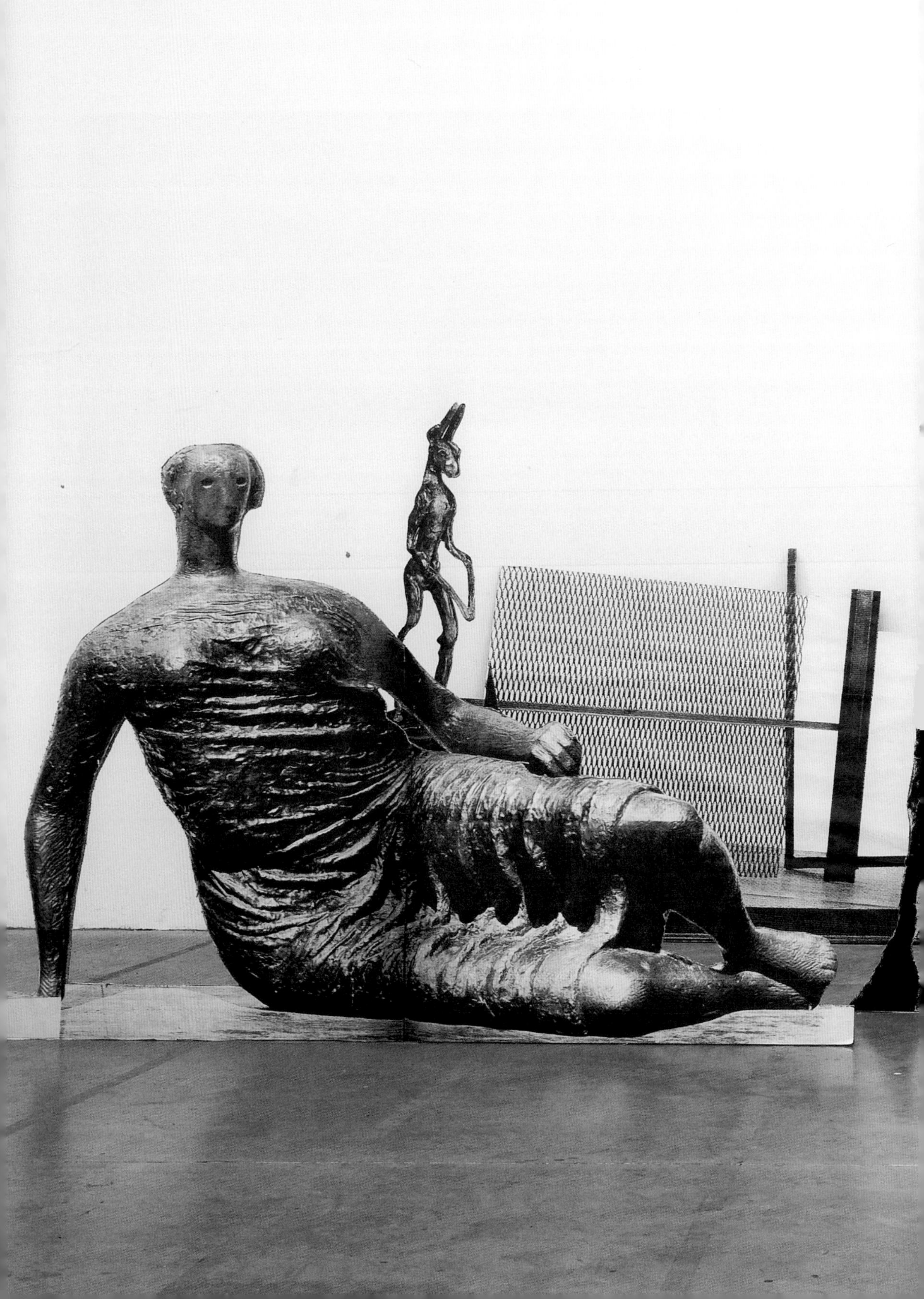

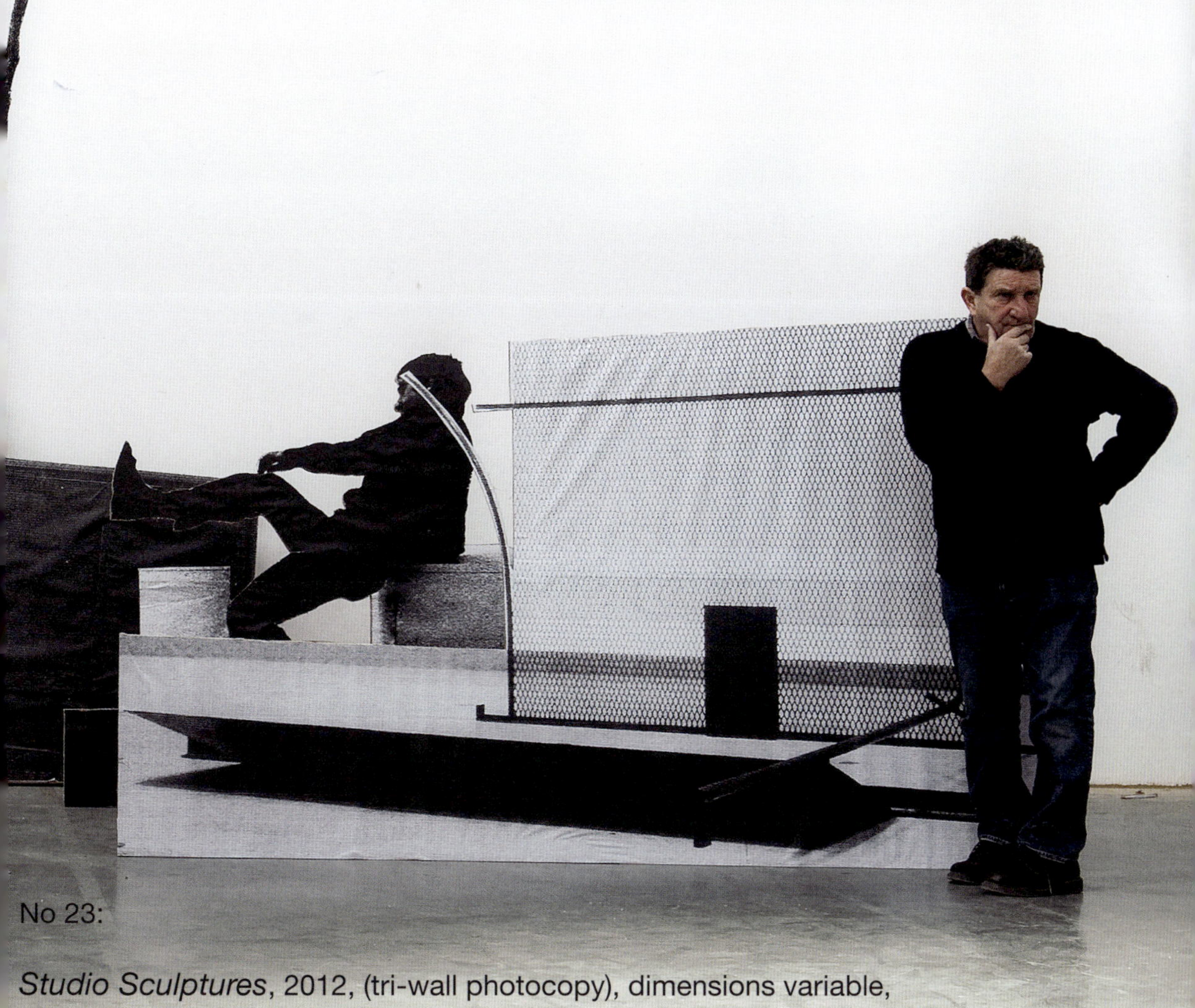

No 23:

Studio Sculptures, 2012, (tri-wall photocopy), dimensions variable,
photographer: Gillian Vaux

Development of a work made in 1969, entitled *Waiter, Waiter there's a
sculpture in my soup*, photo-work. An early reference to Henry Moore.

No 24:

Untitled, 2016, screenprint and acrylic on paper collage on plywood,
152 x 122 cms

A Monoprint.

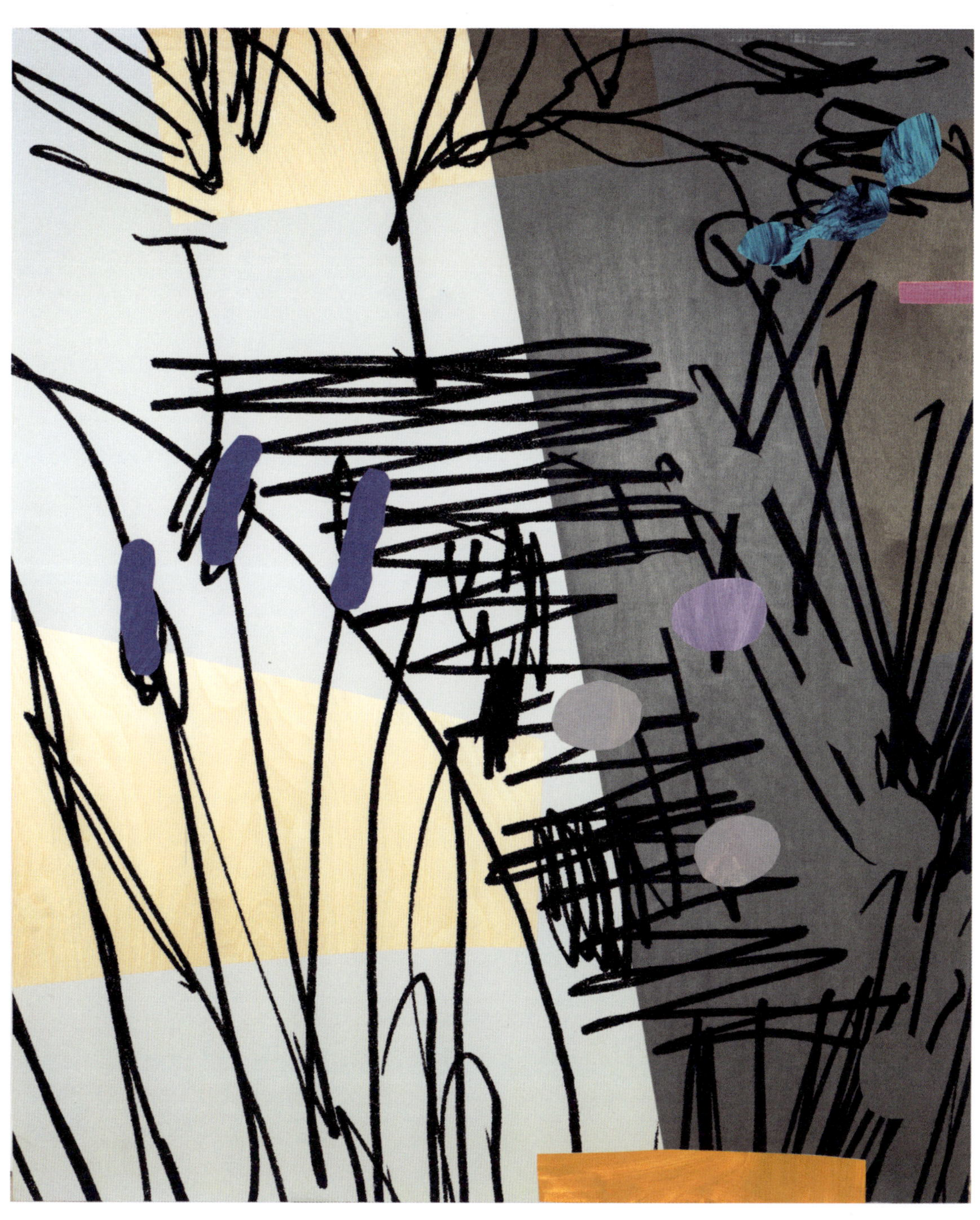

No 25:

Shade Painting: Red, 2016, oil and acrylic on canvas, 265 x 265 cms

A shade painting working backwards from a print of the same subject matter by way of a drawing of the same subject. So now a reverse of the normal procedure of drawing – painting - print.

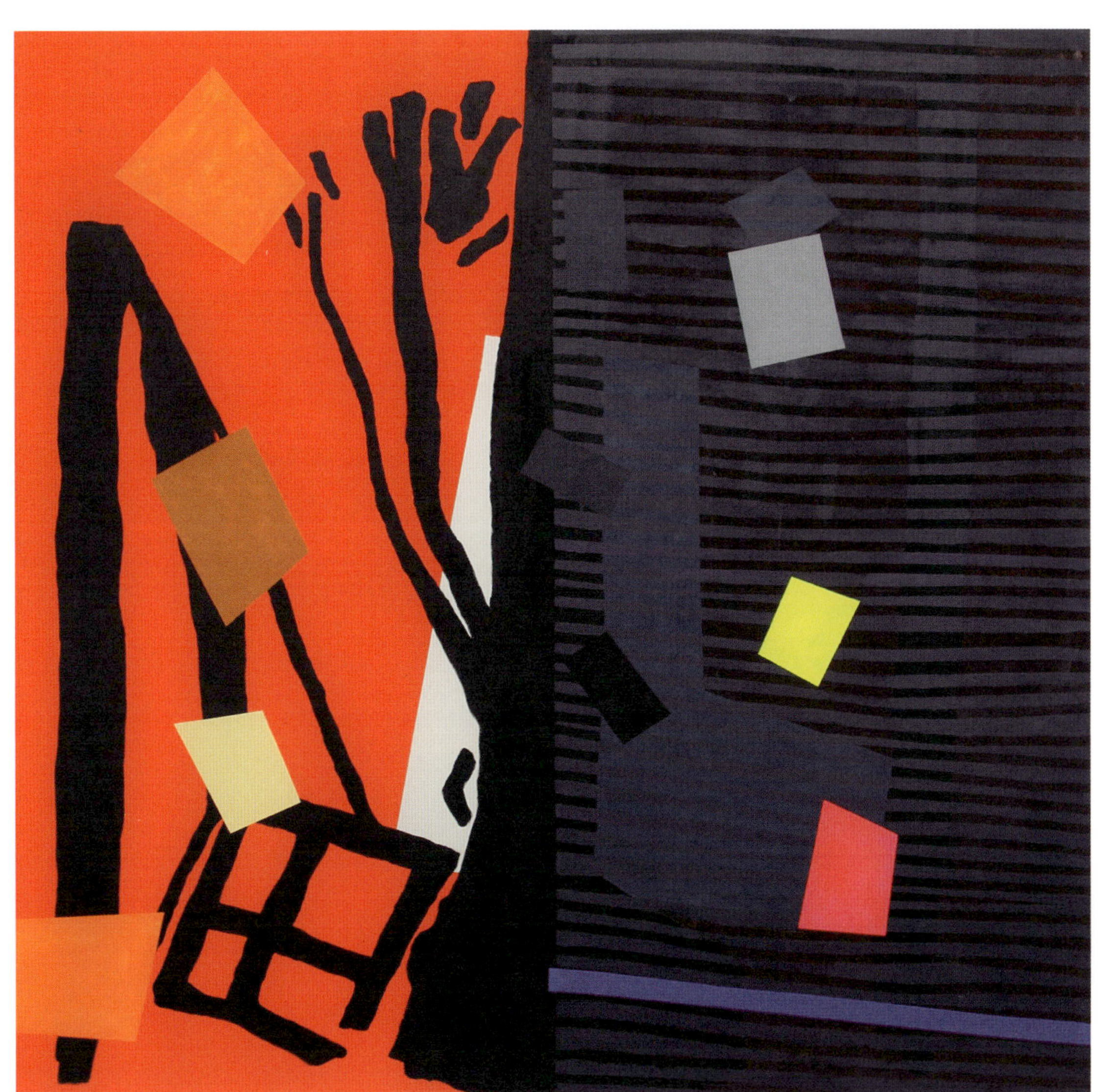

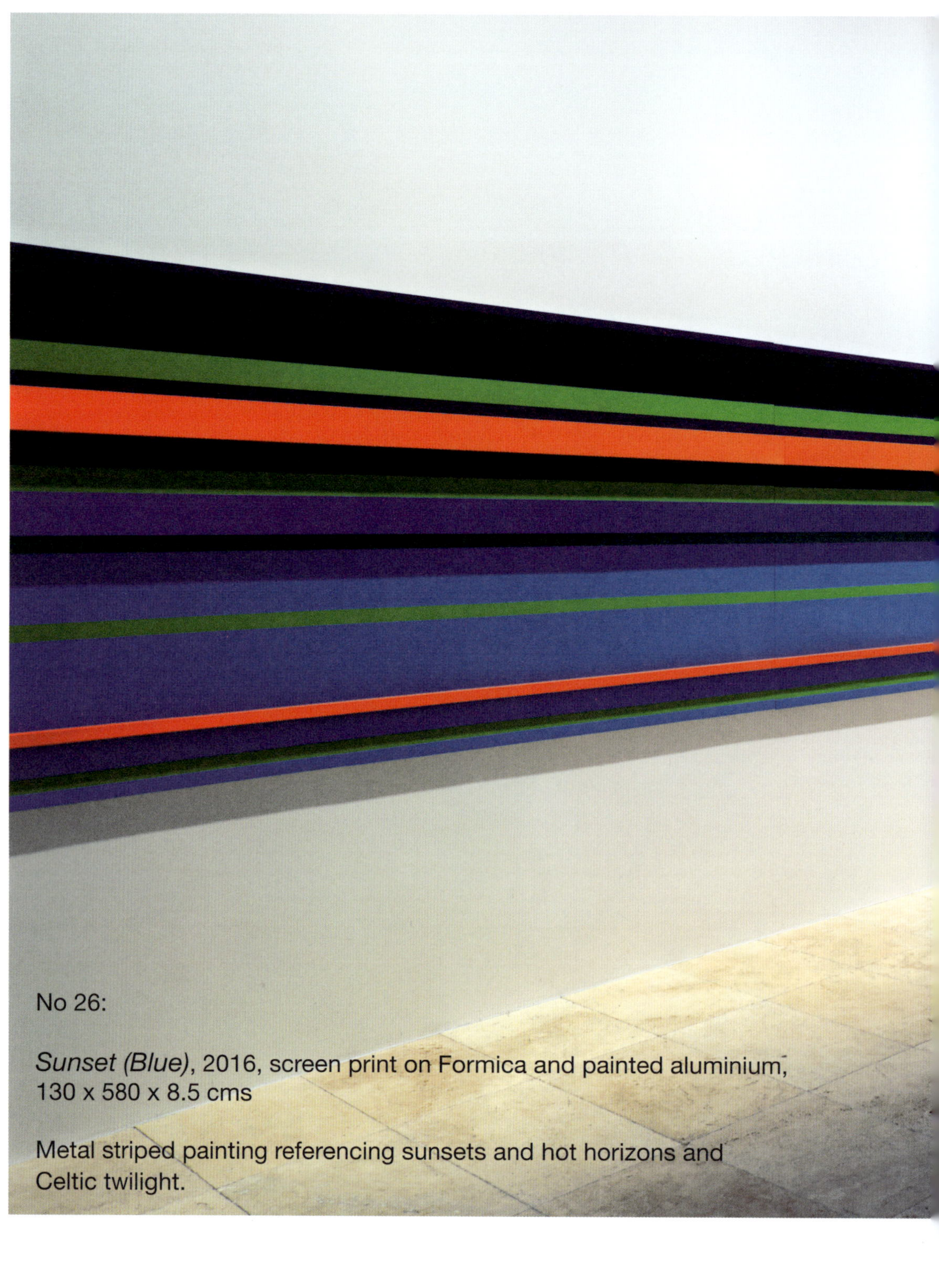

No 26:

Sunset (Blue), 2016, screen print on Formica and painted aluminium, 130 x 580 x 8.5 cms

Metal striped painting referencing sunsets and hot horizons and Celtic twilight.

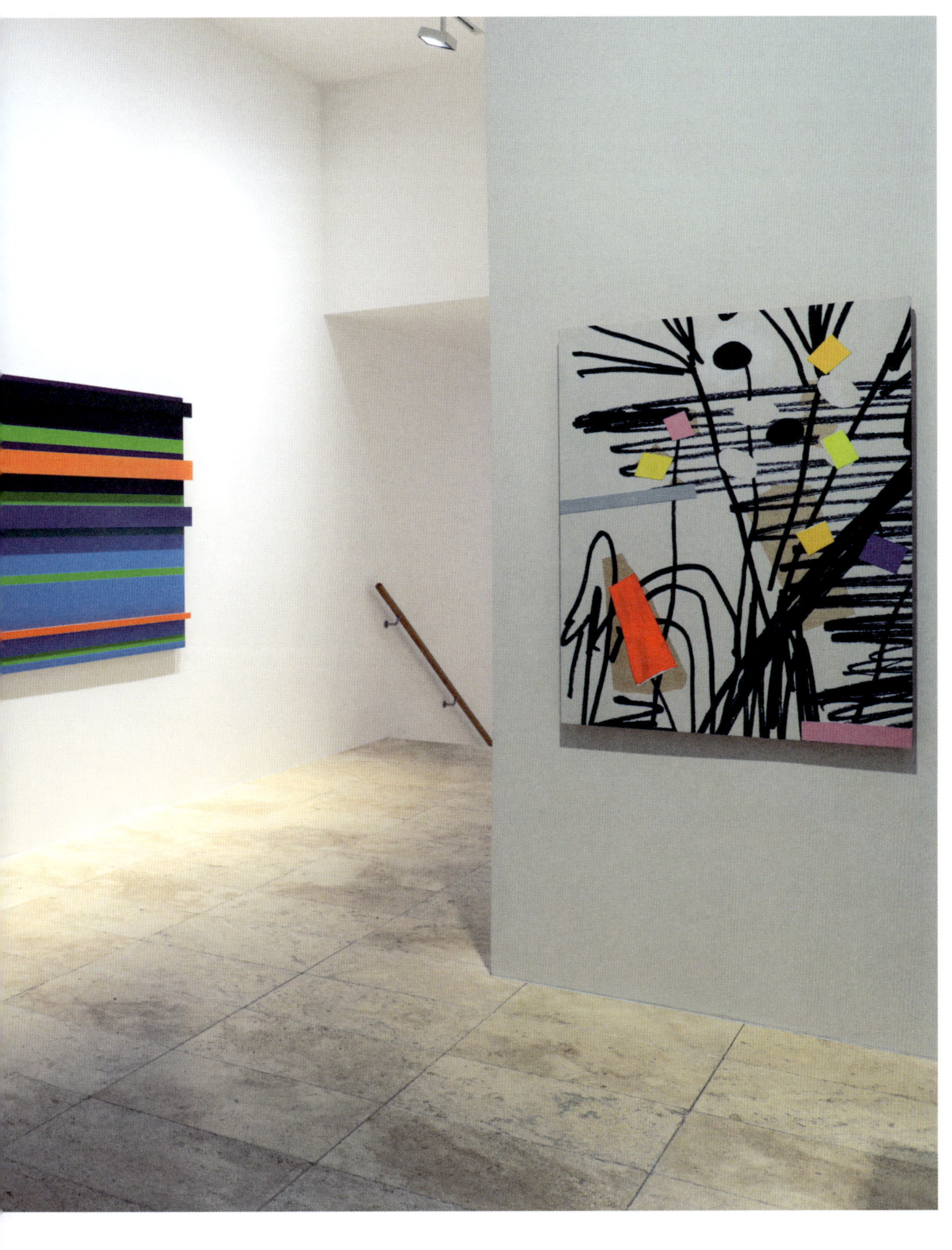

No 27:

Jugs, 2017, ceramic, various sizes

Six jugs on three plinths. Garden works.

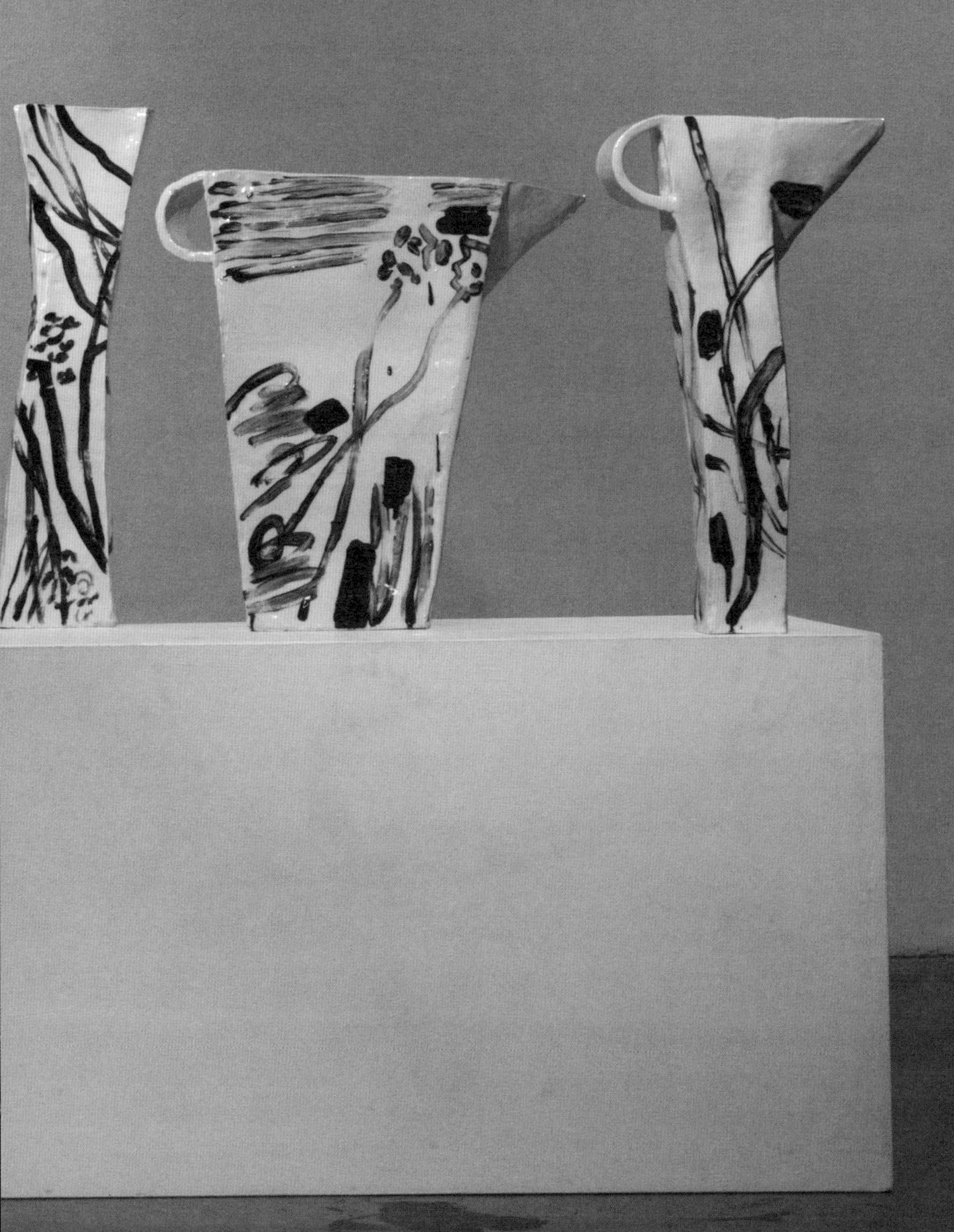

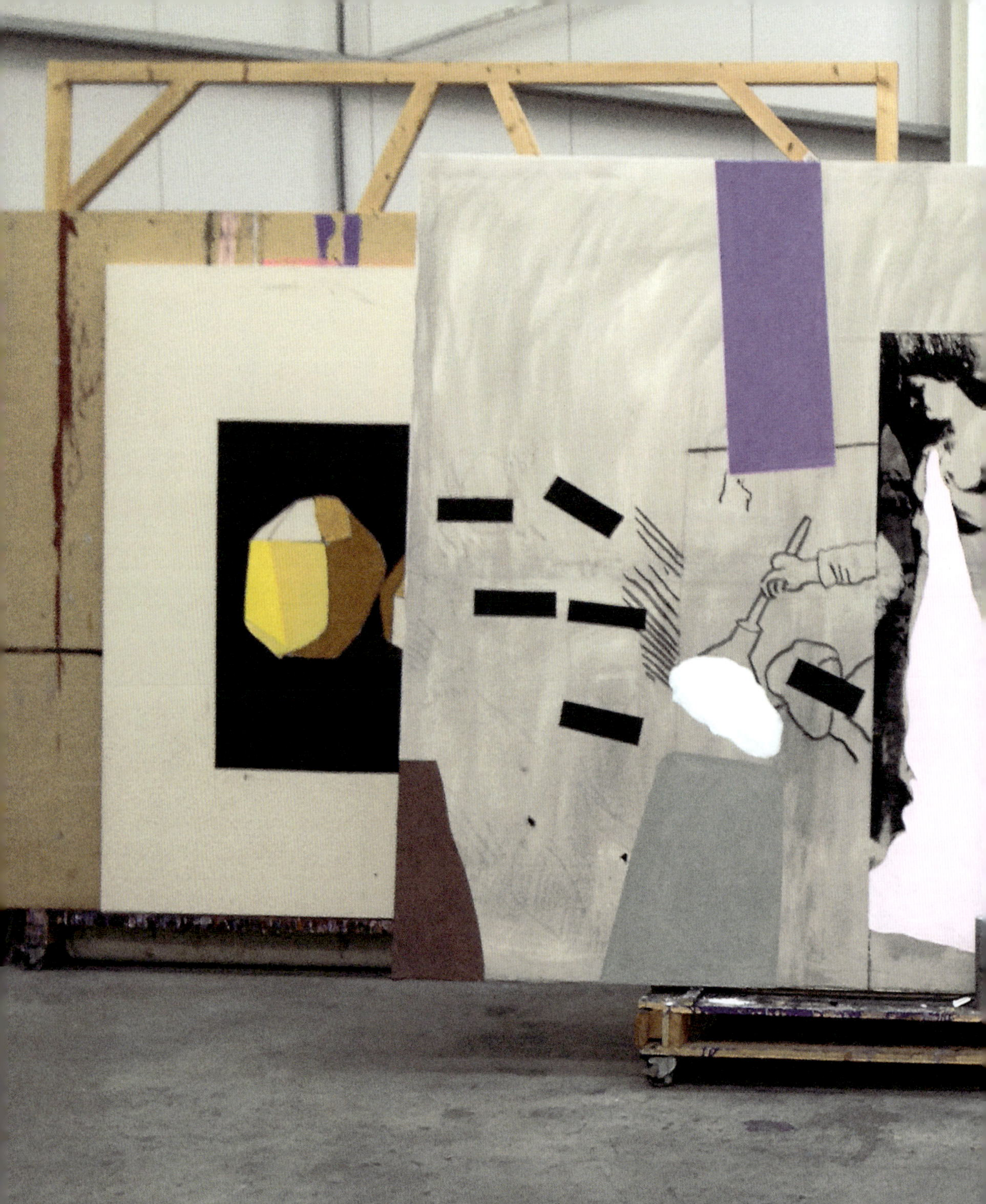

No 28:

Constructed Painting, 2019, oil, screenprint, charcoal and acrylic on canvas, dimensions variable

Constructed painting enacting sculptural procedure, referencing paintings.

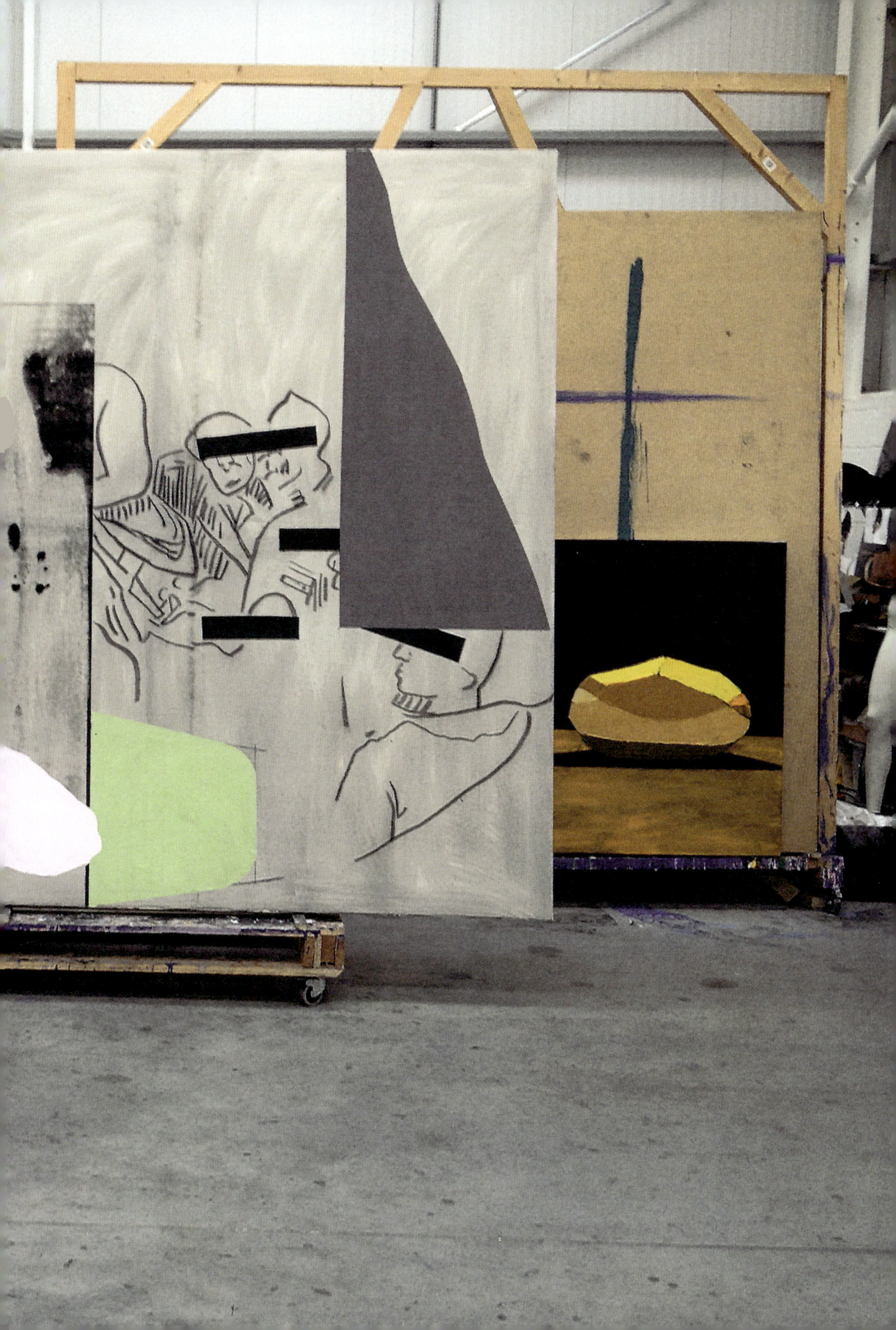

Published 26th April 2019 by

Bernard Jacobson Gallery

To accompany the exhibition

Bruce McLean: Five Decades of Sculpture

26th April – 29th June 2019

Bernard Jacobson Gallery
28 Duke Street St James's
London
SW1Y 6AG

+44 (0) 207 734 3431

www.jacobsongallery.com

ISBN: 978-1-872784-61-8

Cover image: *Fallen Warrior*, 1969, photographer: Dirk Buwalda

Back cover image: *King for a day*, 1969, presented Tate Gallery, Millbank, 11th March 1972, photographer: Dirk Buwalda